A FLEETING MOMENT
IN MY COUNTRY

A FLEETING MOMENT IN MY COUNTRY

The Last Years of the LTTE De-facto State

by

N. MALATHY

Foreword by

Radha d'Souza

CLEAR DAY BOOKS

ISBN: 0-9845255-4-8
       978-0-9845255-4-6
E-book: 978-0-9845255-5-3

In-house editor: Diana G. Collier
Cover: R. Jordan P. Santos

Library of Congress Cataloging-in-Publication Data

Malathy, N.
 A fleeting moment in my country : the last days of the LTTE de-facto state / by N. Malathy ; foreword by Radha d'Souza. -- First edition.
    pages cm
 Includes bibliographical references and index.
 ISBN 978-0-9845255-4-6 (alkaline paper) -- ISBN 0-9845255-4-8 (alkaline paper) -- ISBN 978-0-9845255-5-3 (ebook)
 1. Malathy, N. 2. Sri Lanka--History--Civil War, 1983-2009--Personal narratives. 3. Sri Lanka--History--Civil War, 1983-2009--War work.
 4. Tami_li_la Vitutalaippulikal (Association) 5. Sri Lanka--Politics and government--1978- 6. Human rights--Sri Lanka--Vanni--History--21st century. 7. Vanni (Sri Lanka)--Social conditions--21st century. 8. Vanni (Sri Lanka)--History, Military--21st century. I. Title.
 DS489.86.M36A3 2012
 954.9303'2--dc23
                          2012029780

Clear Day Books
A division of
Clarity Press, Inc.
Ste. 469, 3277 Roswell Rd. NE
Atlanta, GA. 30305 , USA
http://www.claritypress.com

for those who struggled

Table of Contents

Spelling Tamil words

Tamil alphabets to Roman alphabets mapping
The following mapping is used to spell the Tamil words using Roman alphabets. Emphasis is given to maintain the phonetic sound of the Tamil words matched to the English phonetic sounds of the Roman alphabets; thus the one-to-many and the many-to-one mappings of some alphabets.

Short vowels

அ	இ	உ	எ	ஒ	ஐ	ஔ
a	i	u	e	o	ai	ou / ow

Long vowels

ஆ	ஈ	ஊ	ஏ	ஓ		
aa	ii	uu	ee	oo		

Consonants with one-to-one mapping

ட	ப	ம	ய	ர	வ	ஜ	த
d	p	m	y	r	v	j	th

Consonants with one-to-many mapping

க	ச	ற	ஞ	ங	
k / h	s / ch /sh	r / t	gn / n	ng / n	

Consonants with many-to-one mapping

ண	ந	ன	ல	ள	ழ	
n	n	n	l	l	l	

Glossary

General

LTTE	Liberation Tigers of Tamil Eelam
Children's Home	Live-in institutions for needy children
HUDEC	Catholic Humanitarian NGO
Manik Farm	Detention camp for 300,000 Tamil civilians
White van	Euphemism for van used in abductions
GCE O/L & A/L	Lankan government exams for 16 & 18 year olds
UN	United Nations
UNICEF	United Nations Children's Fund
ICRC	International Committee of the Red Cross

2002 ceasefire related terms (see Appendix on history)

CFA	2002 ceasefire agreement
SLMM	Sri Lanka Monitoring Mission
Co-Chair	Combined chair by donor four countries

Some civilian-based institutions in Vanni

CWDR	Centre for Women's Development & Rehabilitation
NESoHR	North East Secretariat on Human Rights
SNE	Statistical Centre for North East
TRO	Tamil Rehabilitation Organization
Senthalir	A children's home run by CWDR
Kurukulam	A children's home run by TRO
Vettimanai	A home for mentally ill women run by CWDR

Some LTTE institutions in Vanni

CWR	Centre for Women's Research
NTT	National Tamil Television
Valankal	LTTE's system of distribution
CPA	Child Protection Authority
Senchoolai	Children's home for girls (bright garden)
Arivuchchoolai	Children's home for boys (knowledge garden)
Anpuchchoolai	Old people's home (love garden)
Mayoori-illam	Home for disabled female LTTE members
Makkal thodarpakam	Offices for liaison with the people

| *Navamarivukkoodam* | Education center for disabled members |

Major LTTE cultural terms

Maaveerar	LTTE member killed in battle (great hero)
Poorali	LTTE member (fighter of justice)
Thiyilum-illam	Cemetery for dead members (home of sleep)
Veeramaranam	Death of a member (hero's death)
Maamanithar	Title of honor to a civilian (great human)

Major commemoration days (thinam) of LTTE

Col. Kiddu thinam	16 January
Annai Poopathi thinam	19 April
Karumpuli thinam	5 July
Thileepan thinam	26 September
Pulenthiran Kumarappa thinam	5 October
Penkal eluchchi thinam	10 October
Maaveerar thinam	27 November

Map

The grey area shown in the rough map used to be a single
administrative unit under the Lankan government called North-East
province. This was the geographic area specified in the Norwegian-
brokered 2002 ceasefire agreement. The homeland claim of the Eelam
Tamils, however, also included the west-coastal district of Puththalam.
Since there was no claim of military control of this district by the
Liberation Tigers of Tamil Eelam (LTTE), this was not included in the
2002 ceasefire agreement.

Vanni is the northern part of the Tamil homeland, excluding
the northernmost Jaffna peninsula. LTTE controlled most but not all of
Vanni at the time of the 2002 ceasefire, and it had its headquarters in
the town of Kilinochchi in Vanni. In this book, Vanni is used to refer
to that part of Vanni that remained in the control of LTTE until the
escalation of war in Vanni in 2006.

In late 2006, immediately after the defeat of LTTE in the
eastern districts of Trincomalee, Batticaloa, and Amparai, the Lankan
government split the North-East province into two provinces, North
and East province.

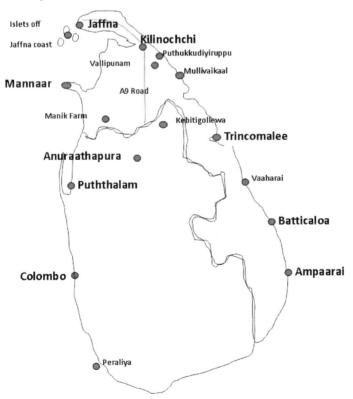

Foreword

A Fleeting Moment in times of cognitive dissonance

Cognitive Dissonance

Some images on the silver screen stay on long after the screening. When the Sri Lankan army proclaimed victory over the Tamils in May 2009 bringing to an end a thirty year struggle for a Tamil homeland, at least for now, TV news channels in India flashed images of Sinhalese coming out in hundreds and distributing sweets on the streets of Colombo in celebration. Alongside the celebratory images there were clips of hundreds of thousands of Tamils herded like cattle into pens in the camps set up after their expulsion from their homeland. I was reminded of images of the Nakba – the Day of Catastrophe – when Palestinians were expelled from their homeland in hundreds of thousands in another time, another place, by another military, an event that occurred before I was born but one that is as alive with us today as it was then. I do not know if Israelis distributed sweets on the streets of Tel Aviv and if they did, there was no TV then to bring the images to people's living rooms. In actuality, I do not know if Sinhalese *really* celebrated in that way or if it was a media-military generated clip. The TV images had not faded in my mind when, out of the blue, I received a request to write the Foreword to *A Fleeting Moment...*

The celebrations on the streets of Colombo died down quickly even on the TV screens and the true character of the Sri Lankan victory became apparent to many. News of assassinations and abductions of Sinhala journalists streamed in before long. Indeed the following year, Sri Lanka's black 'hero' General Sarath Fonseka, who led the ethnic cleansing operations against the Tamils in 2009, was himself arrested and tried. Fonseka had powerful lobbyists though. No less than the US administration declared him to be a 'prisoner of conscience', a victim denied his civil liberties by the Sri Lankan state. The Sri Lankan government was taken aback to find that so soon after winning its own version of the 'war on terror', it was facing charges of genocide against the Tamil people. Western governments which until then had pressured the Sri Lankan government to do more to combat terrorism, now trained their guns against the same government. What are we to make of these very conflicting, contradictory and inconsistent statements and images we hear and see in current affairs?

We live in times of cognitive dissonance.

Next door, India's home minister Palaniappan Chidambaram, ironically himself an Indian Tamil, was sufficiently inspired by the Sri Lanka's military operation against the Tamils to declare that the Indian government would adopt the 'Sri Lankan Solution' to deal with its own insurgencies at home and declared Operation Green Hunt, a military offensive in India's Indigenous belt. As Chidambaram pursued the 'Sri Lankan Solution' for India, the Western media became hysterical about Col. Gaddafi shooting his own people in Libya. The media repeated a single question over and over again: how can any civilised government shoot its own people? The purported government killing of its own people justified NATO's assault on Libya. The Indian's Home Minister's deployment of troops did not warrant the same media attention. What are we to make of all this? That some governments are allowed to wage war against their own people and not others?

In a TV interview aired on 05 December 1996 on the popular US TV magazine show *60 Minutes*- produced by CBS the host and presenter Lesley Stahl questioned the US Secretary of State Madeleine Albright about the effects of sanctions against Iraq amidst reports that thousands of Iraqi children had died because of it. Here is an excerpt from that interview.

> Lesley Stahl on U.S. sanctions against Iraq: "We have heard that a half million children have died. I mean, that's more children than died in Hiroshima. And, you know, is the price worth it?"
> Secretary of State Madeleine Albright: "I think this is a very hard choice, but the price--we think the price is worth it."

UN sanctions against Iraq were imposed from August 1990– just after the UN adopted the Convention on the Rights of the Child in November 1989. The Convention recognises the rights of every child to life, food, water, education, health, identity, freedom and protection. As the sanctions continued and children continued to die in Iraq, the UN debated and expanded on reporting mechanisms for monitoring the convention (1991), included child labour within its scope (1999), and developed optional protocols on child soldiers (2000) and child trafficking (2000).

During this time the UN co-ordinator for humanitarian aid in Iraq, Denis J. Halliday, resigned after thirteen months in Iraq and thirty years in UN service saying:

> Four thousand to five thousand children are dying unnecessarily every month due to the impact of sanctions because of the breakdown of water and sanitation, inadequate diet and the bad internal health situation.[1]

Does common sense not tell us that denying food water and sanitation to an entire population will cause children to die? Why has common sense become so scarce? And, can putting more laws on the statute books make up for lack of common sense?

At the very same moment when the UN Charter was being written, including the chapters on self-determination and decolonisation, the Palestinian nation was being colonised. One of the first actions of the UN after it was formed in 1945 was to approve a plan for the partition of Palestine in order to create Israel. In 1948 Israel declared unilateral independence and resorted to mass expulsion of the Palestinians from their homeland. At that same moment the UN was setting up institutions and mechanisms for decolonisation under the UN Charter. In 1948 the UN envoy to Palestine Folke Bernadotte, a Swedish diplomat and aristocrat, was assassinated by the Zionist organisation LEHI, which was also responsible for the Deir Yassin massacre of Palestinians in April 1949. In May 1949 Israel was admitted to UN membership and described as a 'peace loving country'. These facts are in the public domain for anyone to access. If they are then widely misrepresented or ignored, lack of accurate information is not the sole reason.

The Encyclopaedia of Conflicts Since World War II published by M.E Sharpe describes that book as follows:

> This illustrated reference presents descriptions and analyses of nearly 200 significant post–World War II conflicts around the globe. Organized by region for ease of access, *Encyclopedia of Conflicts Since World War II* provides clear, in-depth explanations of events not covered in such detail in any other reference source. Including more than 180 detailed maps and 150 photos, the encyclopedia highlights the conflicts that dominate today's headlines and the events that changed the course of late twentieth–century history.

Two hundred wars in sixty-six years is an average of three wars a year. The facts are available to anyone who cares to inquire, in neatly indexed and user friendly format that too. Three wars a year occurs after an organisation, the UN, was set up for the *sole* purpose of ending the scourge of wars forever. Surely something must be wrong? The amazing thing is that people the world over continue to believe that UN intervention will bring peace, resistance movements continue to invite UN mediation, or believe that it will act as an honest peace-broker.

It is estimated that during the First World War 5% of the casualties were civilians. Present estimates suggest 75% of the casualties in wars are civilians. Since the authors of the UN Charters wrote in the right of nations to self determination into international law, ethnic conflicts within states have become the single most important source of wars. Have people become suddenly very conscious of their race, religion and ethnicity? Every Euro-American university worth some standing has departments, schools and centers, supported by large research funding grants that specializes in Peace and Security Studies, Conflict Studies, Transitional Justice, International Relations and Politics and a host of other war-related subjects. While characterisation of the state has dominated academic literature and the role of states in wars is routinely analysed there is as yet little attempt to understand the UN theoretically, to characterise its role in the post world war political economy or provide contextual explanations for the persistence of the hiatus between its normative claims and realpolitik of the UN. In the story of the UN and the two hundred wars there are many missing chapters that are yet to be written.

We *do* indeed live in times of cognitive dissonance.

A Fleeting Moment: **A Narrative of Our Times**

A Fleeting Moment is a personal narrative of what the author has witnessed firsthand when she went to Vanni in the Tamil homeland in Sri Lanka as a volunteer to do her bit, as it were, to make the Oslo peace accord brokered by Norway work. She was clearly not prepared for the turn that events took while there. Like so many people in Africa, Asia, Latin America and Middle East, Malathy too believed that a UN backed peace accord would bring order, peace, and justice to her people. Malathy's journey through the realities of the peace process on the ground and the eventual fate of the Tamils is an important story for all to digest. Too many Third World nations are engulfed in strife and civil wars, all too swiftly becoming targets of military operations undertaken not just by their state but by external powers. Then they are further victimized by interpretations of the conflict from foreign media echoing the foreign policies of their states. For people in the Euro-American nations Malathy's thoughtfulness and the "on-the'ground" nature of her account is an invitation to seriously and without intermediation review the internal climate created by one such resisting group, and to reflect further on the legitimacy of their grievances, and hopefully thereby come to question their assumptions and beliefs about the international order and what their states do in their name. The desire to make sense of the traumatic events that have overtaken the Tamil nation permeates Malathy's narrative in the book. The issues she raises in the book transcend specific questions related to Tamil self-determination.

Malathy ends her extraordinary account of the last four years of the LTTE with the observation:

> Tamils can resolve the riddles thrust in their face only by grasping this interdependent global politico-military-economic sphere and its decisive influence on the outcome of the LTTE campaign.

If we put the Tamil struggle for homeland in perspective by locating it in the context of the militarism and ethnic conflicts of post World War era, (the memory of Rwanda is still raw in our minds), the significance of her observations can be extended by rephrasing it thus:

> *Oppressed nations* can resolve the riddles thrust in their faces only by grasping this interdependent global-politico-military- economic-*environmental* sphere and its decisive influence on the outcome of *their struggles for independence and freedom.*

Further, the book concludes:

> Many other nations have achieved their independence [...] because the politico-economic military sphere was conducive.

Malathy is careful not to overstep the remit she was working within and the limits that a personal narrative imposes upon her. The reader has no such remit and is free to ponder the wider significance of the Tamil struggle to ask 'what can we learn from this'? In the light of the post-independence experiences of Third World states, call it neo-colonialism, call it dependency or whatever, we may also add:

> Many other nations achieved their goal of statehood because they willingly mistook statehood for freedom and self-determination and believed that once statehood was achieved, democracy and freedom would co-

exist peacefully with imperialism and globalized neoliberalism.

Without public demand for a genuine internationalism against the oppressive global order and its institutions, and without resistance movements' understanding of the international stew of interests in which their struggles are inescapably embedded, domestic/national and local movements tend to either get hijacked or co-opted or defeated.

This book reveals the processes by which the international view of the 'facts' becomes socially constructed and how dominant institutions of power and authority give purchase to one type of facts and not others. The LTTE was in no position to put forth its version of the facts as effectively as UN institutions or Western NGOs, while the orientations of these were impacted by major state and global economic actors' views of their own self-interest.[2]

It is often assumed that 'seeing' social events/occurrences is analogous to biological 'seeing'. The physical eye is the same for everyone and operates similarly even in social epidemiology because of its grounding in physiology. Social facts are invariably grounded in particular social contexts and always informed by the histories, geographies, language and grammar, concepts and ideologies of the society to which the fact relates. Taken out of its social context a fact can be truth or falsehood or neither or a bit of both. Dominant economic and political interests are able to privilege some aspects or types of de-contextualised facts over others because of their positions of influence and control within institutions and present a distorted reality to the world.

When the global public lacks information or grounding in the local context we tend to fill the missing knowledge gaps by substituting our own social moorings, and so we become receptive to suggestions by states and other actors from comparable social and cultural locations as ourselves. We open ourselves up to manipulation by states and other actors who are fully aware of how facts on the ground might be tuned to play to uninformed global "common sense", to positive or negative ends. Many well intentioned people who opt to work for NGOs and intergovernmental organisations believe they serve the common good and fail to recognise the role of NGOs and intergovernmental as key actors in neoliberal globalisation because their education and training does not equip them to interrogate the normative claims of the organisations they work for. Facts are produced in bureaucratic contexts where the person seeing has been instructed on what they should see by the rules of the organisation passed down through an organisational hierarchy, and heavily indebted to state or funder perspective. Facts produced within bureaucratic contexts serve the interests of those who command the organisations.

Modern institutions are founded on positive law i.e. law that relies on doctrinal definitions stripped of social context. This feature of modern law makes it applicable universally as if local contexts, histories and geographies are irrelevant. The abstract doctrinal nature of modern law renders the institutional underpinnings of society opaque and conceals the interests and actors it serves. Modern institutions introduce a hiatus between individual conscience and institutional norms and invite us to behave as if we were embodiments of rules. The consequences are often tragic as the struggle for Tamil homeland shows.

The struggle for a Tamil homeland was a struggle to restore the governance over the lives of the Tamil people reflecting their unity of place, history, culture and language, and to develop viable economic conditions for life. However their struggle occurred in a global context that fragments collectives and even sovereign states and inserts each aspect of the lives of individuals into a different legal and institutional framework each with its own bureaucracy and rule makers. There is no cosmology, no ancestors, no history, no transcendental authority for ethics in the global order that frames our institutional lives. Thus we are presented with the paradox of our times: the severance of the notion of a homeland from the cluster of ideas that make up our traditions as developed from our collective lives living on our lands. We can have a homeland, if at all, only if we are willing to accept a delegated role within a global hierarchy of power and operate as a unit of governance over a territory recognised by global powers. This tension between the idea of a place based 'homeland' and placeless institutions is a subtext that runs throughout the book. Told as a personal narrative the tension is deeply moving.

There is a Tamil proverb that says the voices of destitute cannot reach royal audience halls (agati chol ambalam eraadu). Here, the problem is not of amplification of the voice or deafness of those gathered in royal halls. Rather, the cries of the destitute become inaudible because the institutional walls of audience halls are sound proofed. The book illustrates how the sound-proofing is achieved in the modern context.

'Soft Power', 'Soft Law' and an Iron Fist

Readers will realise as they go through these pages that the peace process was the beginning of the end of the Tamil struggle for a homeland. The struggle for a Tamil homeland was not wanting in sustained popular support, heroism and courage, discipline or sacrifices. The struggle got mired in the peace process. The peace process softened up the resistance of a war weary nation. It engaged with the resistance on social standards, including human rights, demanding from it the same universal standards as a state with full membership of the UN; but it did so without recognising the demand for statehood. In other words, it was a demand to live up to high ethical standards without the institutional preconditions for it. Ceasar's wife must be above suspicion but without the privileges of power and wealth due to Ceasar's wife.

The demand for international social and cultural standards from the LTTE without statehood enabled the peacemakers and international media to discredit the claims of the entire Tamil nation for self-determination for their homeland. The discrediting occurred in a context where so many full-fledged member-states of the UN continued to have appalling human rights records including, one may add, the prison-industrial complexes and the widespread and controversial uses of the death penalty in the US. There are no means by which one can contextualise the standards of human rights within resistance movements or compare them against the states that are standard bearers for human rights.

The peace process prepared an international climate of opinion favourable to the military operation by discrediting the Tamil claim for the right to a homeland and by putting organised Tamil resistance on hold. After the softening up was achieved the peace makers packed up and left, leaving the ground open for a full scale military operation by the Sri Lankan state. When the military offensive was underway there was very little international intervention. Once the military 'victory' over the Tamils was complete the peace makers were back at work, this time to put the Sri Lankan state on the dock for crimes against the Tamils. The account of the use of 'soft law' and 'soft power' in conjunction with militarism and 'hard law' in the book is a pattern that is not limited to Sri Lanka; it can be seen in many other struggles around us today.

The origin of 'soft law' lies in the UN Charter. Before formation of the UN, international law was almost entirely about law governing political relations between states and based on treaties or customary state practices. The UN Charter for the first time gave the UN a vastly expanded role in economic, social and cultural spheres. The UN Charter distributes power through the different political and economic organs created under the Charter. Political power is shared primarily between the Security Council and the General Assembly. The Security Council is the only organ that has powers to enforce decisions, intervene militarily, arbitrate or mediate in disputes and impose political and economic sanctions. The Security Council is in effect controlled by the Big Five, by the veto powers who are all victors in the two preceding world wars. In contrast the General Assembly comprises all member states. The powers of the General Assembly are recommendatory and non-binding. The General Assembly's main task is to develop non-binding legal instruments on social, cultural and political issues – i.e. develop 'soft law' and persuade states to adopt them. Since the formation of the UN Third World states have been included in the process of developing 'soft law' instruments on various social and cultural issues. The most important role of 'soft law' instruments is to guide Third World states into behaving in particular ways, to harmonise law across countries on social, cultural and economic matters, and to create the institutional infrastructures that make global governance possible. At the same time the dominance of the Security Council ensures that Third World states remain subordinate to the Allies. The Big Five govern and the Third World states are governed.

When social movements on the ground demand international intervention, which they do all too frequently, they do so because the primary focus of their struggle is domestic and directed against their own states and governments. Social movements and resistance movements take international norms that are developed as non-binding instruments at face value. They believe that because their states are subordinate to the Big Five appealing to the higher authority of the Big Five will bring them justice. What is often overlooked is that while it is true that appealing to the Big Five enables international interventions, whether the intervention can bring them justice remains questionable. This much had become clear to many people and movements in the course of the many proxy wars that characterised the Cold War. However, the continued failure to theorise or contextualise the UN and recognise it for what it is—a creature of the victorious Allies in the World Wars—and understand the ways in which the UN institutionalises the dominant economic and political powers in the post World War order means people and social movements are often unprepared for the 'soft power' that has come to characterise the post Cold War, globalisation era.

'Soft power', a phrase coined by Joseph Nye Jr., an ideologue of neo-liberalism closely associated with the Clinton Administration in the US, harnesses a wide range of civil society organisations including academia, NGOs, voluntary organisations, research organisations and campaign groups to serve a concerted political agenda set by the powers that be. Thus 'rolling back the state' under globalisation is not limited to its role in domestic management of the local economy alone, as many anti-globalisations movements suppose, but includes 'rolling back the state' from politics, education, law, and social and economic provisioning. What is rolled in, instead, are the international NGOs, the aid agencies, academic institutions, legal teams and much more. The reader will read about the role of eminent academics as well as NGOs in the book. The mobilisation of civil society groups for a political agenda has the appearance of democratisation, but only that. As Third World states are visibly repressive, the deployment of 'soft power' appeals to social movements. What is often forgotten is that not just citizens but internal nations have rights, and breaches of those rights gives peoples the moral and international legal authority to challenge the state. People cannot make any claims against NGOs like Amnesty International or Oxfam referred to in the book. Yet in the neoliberal era such organisations are integral to the way 'soft power' operates. There is a complex and often invisible interplay of state and non-state actors in global governance.

Far too many contemporary struggles for justice demonstrate exemplary organisational skills, resistance and creativity against their states but fail to grasp the true character of the international order within which the subjugation of Third World states themselves as well as their internal peoples occur, and the external interests that come into play when differences between the state and citizens are played out in the international context. Despite the two hundred wars and the Palestinian, Kashmiri, Chechen and a host of other resistance movement experiences, people in the Third World continue to see the UN as a neutral, objective peacemaker in domestic conflicts. Similarly, there have been many global protest movements since the end of the Cold War against international economic organisations like the World Bank, or IMF or the WTO. There is a universal perception among global protest movements that the standard setting organisations like the UNICEF or the World Health Organisation, or the UN Human Rights Council have a positive role to play as the highest and only existing mechanisms purporting to represent global needs with impartiality. They fail to see the UN system in its totality and understand the complementary roles that international economic organisations like the WTO or World Bank and the international standard setting organisations, *both*, play within the global system. Indeed international economic organisations like the World Bank and the WTO view standard setting organisations like the WHO or UNHCR as necessary components of the global economy because social and cultural standards create 'level playing fields' for economic actors and help in 'risk management'. The UN system itself is nonetheless and inescapably a reflection of and indeed often the amphitheatre for testing and asserting the global strength of its major players, and consequently its institutions lend themselves to becoming the 'soft power' for the 'iron fist' that holds the UN system together.

It is pertinent to ask why the Sinhalese state became vulnerable internationally precisely at its moment of victory, having enjoyed US and thereby UN support for so long? What does it mean that the Tamils, now defeated, seem set at last to enjoy the sympathy of the global community? As one of the most significant movements since the end of the Vietnam War the Tamil struggle merits deeper analysis. While this Foreword cannot undertake an evaluation of the LTTE or the struggle for a Tamil homeland, it is to be hoped that such an objective evaluation can indeed take place. The tragedy of our times is that vast majority of people who want a just and peaceful world and are willing to work for it can no longer tell the difference between perpetrators and victims or between decisions emanating from the highest seats of global power legitimated by international law and global justice. This book contributes in a small way to help us differentiate between the two in these times of cognitive dissonance.

Radha D'Souza
London, August 2012.

A FLEETING MOMENT
IN MY COUNTRY

Preface

It was a fleeting moment in one's life, but it was also the most memorable. And then it was gone, all traces of it completely wiped out. That tumultuous end is now making world history as an example of defeating terrorism and as an example of unreported genocide. I was a spectator with a preferential seat. What I saw in that fleeting moment is what I record here. This book is a firsthand account of the four years I worked as a volunteer in Vanni in northern Sri Lanka, which was under the control of the LTTE until its defeat in 2009.

The defeat of the LTTE in Mullivaikaal in May 2009 is a landmark moment in the history of armed struggles by non-state actors, and thus of immense importance. It will continue to be studied for a long time from many angles. This book may be of some value for such studies. My main motivation for writing this record, however, is the conviction that recording history is an important aspect of the survival of a people. I believe I not only had a unique experience, but also, because of my citizenship in New Zealand, I have a unique opportunity to write about it without the security threat faced by others who experienced the same.

I am a member of the Tamil Diaspora, and I had lived in New Zealand for more than thirty years prior to spending this period in Vanni. I had been an activist in New Zealand for a few years, working towards what I told myself would be "peace" on that island. I am at heart a social activist, and the experimental Vanni society of the LTTE under the 2002 ceasefire was inviting. Thus, I made two short trips, a six-week-long trip at the end 2002 and a three-month-long trip starting in April 2004, to investigate if I had a role to play in Vanni. Drawn to Vanni, in March 2005 I made my long-term move. I spent four years in the Vanni of the LTTE, from 2005 until 2009. This period was marked by the gradual weakening of the 2002 Norwegian-brokered ceasefire, which eventually led to the brutal war in which the LTTE was defeated and its leadership killed or imprisoned.

During this period I worked with key LTTE leaders and in key institutions in Vanni, including a human rights body—North East Secretariat on Human Rights (NESoHR), the LTTE Peace Secretariat, a women's organization—the Centre for Women's Development & Rehabilitation (CWDR), and an orphanage. My experiences spanned working with the LTTE to release child soldiers, preparing documentation for peace talks for the same body, documenting for NESoHR the human rights violations by the Lankan Military, and working on a project to raise awareness of domestic violence.

I left Vanni during the last phase of the war, in March 2009, from Mullivaikaal by an International Committee of the Red Cross (ICRC) ship. I was detained by the Lankan Military in the Manik Farm camp with the rest of the 300,000 Tamils who had walked out of the war zone. The war ended in May 2009 with the defeat of the LTTE, two months after I left Mullivaikaal and while I was detained in the Manik Farm camp. I got out of the Manik Farm camp and out of Sri Lanka later in 2009.

In this record, I have assumed the reader's knowledge of the prior history of the struggle of the Tamil people in Sri Lanka. I would urge those readers who lack this knowledge to read the appendix on that history included here before reading the main text. One point that must be emphasized is that by the time of the Norwegian-brokered 2002 ceasefire agreement between the Lankan government and the LTTE, the people had already faced thirty years of war and loss.

My initial exposure in Vanni was to destitute children who were cared for in orphanages under LTTE control as well as in other child-based institutions. These institutions were part of the efforts to ameliorate the conditions resulting from three decades of war. One of my early projects during my second visit was to highlight the many aspects of war-affected children, bar the child soldier issue. This sets the scene for my later work specifically with the child soldier issue. One such child-based institution in Vanni was Senchoolai, under the management of a senior female LTTE member, Janani. Both Janani and Senchoolai are legends in the history of the LTTE. My association with this institution began during my very first visit and continued throughout. I have dedicated a whole chapter to describe the achievements and the heartaches of this institution under Janani.

When I started to work in the human rights body, NESoHR, it was a continuation of my earlier work with destitute children, because at that time NESoHR was also dealing mostly with child soldiers. This body was an offshoot of the 2002 peace process. However, I defined my own role within this organization as the documentation person and set about recording the atrocities against the Tamil people that had gone on until then. There was so much that needed to be recorded, including land confiscation, mass massacres and disappearances, and deliberate demographic changes. As time progressed, I also found myself recording current atrocities.

Gradually I was drawn into the LTTE Peace Secretariat circle. Working with the LTTE Peace Secretariat gave me the opportunity to understand the complex child soldier issue. I was drawn into this prickly issue, and I describe this extensively in the book. The reader will come to understand why the child soldier issue was a persistent problem within the LTTE and how this issue became a hot topic on the international scene.

When I worked in NESoHR, I had opportunities to interact with some representatives from the West who visited Vanni. Later at the LTTE Peace Secretariat, I had more opportunities to observe interactions with all types of international agencies—the peacemakers, the UN, and others bodies. I also interacted extensively with UNICEF over the child soldier issue, and this, too, added to my developing perspective on the international position. Due to the type of work I did at the Peace Secretariat, I also closely followed the international media reports at this time about the peace process and the stance of these same Western agencies on this topic. I attempt to give a factual firsthand description based on my direct experience about the positioning of various international agencies in Vanni.

To understand Vanni under the LTTE is also to understand the extensive and unique rituals practiced there. These rituals instituted by the LTTE were followed by everyone and were well entrenched. They were mostly centered on LTTE members who had been killed in action. Pervasive symbols and icons, including martyrs' graveyards and the emotional connection of the people to these, are important aspects of Vanni culture. The Vanni media was another important aspect of its social fabric. There were numerous media outlets, but three dominated the daily lives of the people—*Eelnaatham* daily newspaper, Pulikalin-kural radio service, and the National Tamil Television (NTT), the national television. All of them came under attack from the Lankan authorities. Vanni society, especially the LTTE section of it, engaged in lively debates on many issues, and this is one of the aspects of Vanni I very much enjoyed. Compulsory one per family recruitment and the Cricket World Cup created lively debates. Though compulsory recruitment itself was not debated publicly, many of its flow-on effects were.

I went to Vanni dreaming of working on women's issues, but I had the chance to do so too late—not until 2008. Yet, I studied the field. I was initially disappointed, but as time went by I was awestruck by the interconnected female culture that was active in the public space and on the lookout for the welfare of other women. It was a unique form of feminism. Of all the losses Tamils are facing due to the destruction of this Vanni, it is the loss of what was gained in this area that pains me most.

The 2002 ceasefire brought many international agencies into Vanni. Vanni society was thus coloured by LTTE institutions, Lankan institutions, and international agencies. All of these bodies had many channels of interaction, creating a political cum economic life in Vanni that yet was dominated by the LTTE philosophy. The growth of many old institutions and the sprouting of many new institutions under the LTTE was the hallmark of the early ceasefire period. I endeavour to give a sense of these developments to the reader.

My experience of multiple displacements, starting in late 2008 and ending in Mullivaikaal, and my exit from the war zone by ICRC ship, only to be interned in gruesome UN-supported camps, completed my four-year Vanni experience.

Due to the pace of work, and later due to the constant threat of attacks, I do not think I managed to decipher the experiential knowledge I had gained during this period. Once safely back in New Zealand, reflection was possible. I was then able to fit together perfectly all of the knowledge I had gained, like a jigsaw puzzle. I share this personal enlightenment in the final chapter.

The recording of these life experiences was made possible by the many who contributed to make that experience happen. Primary contributors to my experiences recorded here are the people of Vanni, who struggled on bravely against the entire world. Any credit for this book is entirely theirs. I also thank my family and my friends for their suggestions and corrections.

1

The girl in the
makkal thodarpakam

Houses in hot climates have an open veranda so that one can enjoy the fresh breeze while sitting in the shade of a roof. So did the house I would walk or drive past almost every day for the next four years, because it was right next to the Peace Secretariat of the Liberation Tigers of Tamil Eelam (LTTE) in Kilinochchi.

The open yard in front of the veranda was sandy and large. It was also well shaded by trees, mostly mango trees. The sand was loose like beach sand and was brownish-white, ideal for children to play with. People, mainly women, sat in the shade of the trees, squatting on the sandy ground. Children were playing with the sand or running around. A few more people, who preferred the tidy veranda to the sand, were seated on the veranda floor. Some were hanging their legs over the edge of the veranda, while others sat cross-legged. One could hear noises of activity coming from inside the house.

This was a *makkal thodarpakam* of the LTTE. These were offices of the LTTE which were the first port of call for civilians wanting something from the LTTE or wishing to make a complaint about LTTE actions. The few men there either wore dark trousers or a sarong and short-sleeved shirt. All of the older women were *saree* clad, while the younger ones were wearing a knee-length skirt and a top. The only sign that gave away the fact that it was an LTTE office was the typical female LTTE attire worn by those women involved in civil duties. This included dark pants and a light-coloured, loosely-fitting shirt with a belt worn over it. LTTE men carrying out civil duties were hardly distinguishable from the civilian men. One man sat behind a table on the verandah. In front of him were two chairs. A woman sat on one of the chairs, talking to the man. When the woman finished her business the next woman was called upon.

Accompanying this second woman, about to meet the officer at the table, was the woman's sixteen year old daughter and a toddler in the woman's arms. They had come by bus from Jaffna to collect the girl's school results certificate that was held by a division of the LTTE. The girl had completed her schooling while being an LTTE member. She had been released under a UN-sponsored Action Plan signed in 2003 to release child soldiers. The woman and her daughter took their seats in front of the man. As the man at the desk started to give instructions on how they may proceed to obtain the certificate, the teenager started to say something in an adamant tone, looking down at the floor all the time.

"I want to stay here. I do not want to come back home."

The place went silent as everyone stopped their chatter and listened more attentively. What the girl had just said implied that she wanted to be with the LTTE and that she did not want to return with her mother to Jaffna. To this the mother retorted in outrage as her voice started to break and tears swelled in her eyes.

"Is this why you brought me here, all the way from Jaffna?"

The show of hurt and outrage rather than surprise in the mother's voice gave away something. It showed that the girl's unwillingness to stay with the family after her release from the LTTE was already known to the mother. The girl's face tightened. She would not even look up. The mother and daughter continued to exchange words in the same tone for a while, with the girl speaking softly, all the while looking down at the floor, and the teary mother shouting back. The man at the table interrupted their tense conversation and said to the mother,

"You can leave her at the education center here, if you like."

The man was referring to the education center run by a local NGO— the Tamil Rehabilitation Organization (TRO)—that was partly funded by UNICEF to run this specific center. It was one of the off-shoots of the UN sponsored 2003 Action Plan to release child soldiers.

In the end, the outraged mother came to the conclusion that her daughter would not go back with her. She then demanded the gold chain worn by the girl, which the girl promptly removed and gave to her mother. The mother demanded the girl's earrings too. She was too angry now even to speak properly. Some women seated under the trees appealed to the mother to leave the earrings on the girl.

With whatever she removed from her teenage daughter, she walked off carrying the toddler and crying aloud,

"What will I tell my husband now? He is going to be in a rage."

This story unfolded in early 2004. What happened to this teenage girl, who would have been placed at the education center? Did the parents persist and eventually succeed in getting her released prior to the closure of the A9 route to Jaffna? If they failed, then she most certainly would have fought in the war from 2006 onwards. Did she die in frontline duty? Did she escape the war zone in May 2009, and was she then interned somewhere in the government detention centers? Was she later released? Was she one of those who was sexually abused by the Lankan Military and eventually executed? Did she manage to escape by bribing her way out, as some did? Hers is just one story in the gigantic web of tragic stories that has engulfed the people of Tamil Eelam.[1]

The many, varied, and ever-multiplying media in Vanni used to lead the way in telling the stories of the people of Vanni during this time. However, the story of that girl in the *makkal thodarpakam,* or anything like it, never appeared in the Vanni media. The outside media would see this girl's story as part of the child soldier blot slapped on the LTTE. In reality, however, what was happening inside Vanni was not a specifically child soldier phenomenon. It was the phenomenon of recruitment with a triangular set of forces acting at its innermost level: the LTTE with its appetite for recruitment, the young person with idealism and other conflicting pulls, and the family, who feels a sense of loss when one of their young members joins the LTTE. UN instruments and resolutions on child soldiers were applied to this inner sociological current, creating a very negative picture of the LTTE child-soldier phenomenon. All of this I did not know when I observed the event in that *makkal thodarpakam.* But it was unique for an expatriate Tamil because it was a spontaneous event and not one organized by the LTTE for a member of the Diaspora.

How did I come to see it? It was April 2004 and my second three-month-long visit to Kilinochchi had just started. My first visit, which was a much shorter one and very quiet with no meetings of LTTE dignitaries, was at the end of 2002. A one-month stay at the Senchoolai children's home in the middle of Vallipunam jungle was the highlight of that visit. This second visit in 2004 was to begin, on the urging of a few friends in the Diaspora, with an audience with Thamilselvan, the political head of the LTTE. Not surprisingly, no one in the political headquarters knew me except that I had an introductory email from Jeyakumar. A Diaspora Tamil from Australia, Jeyakumar died of natural causes in 2007 and was honoured by the LTTE with the *Maamanithar* title. After being shunted around a little bit by the people at the political headquarters, I was asked to wait at the *makkal thodarpakam* while they decided what to do with me. That is how I came to watch the above drama unfold in the *makkal thodarpakam.*

2

Castaway children

After waiting at the *makkal thodarpakam* for two hours, I was granted an audience first with Pulitheevan, the Secretary General of the LTTE Peace Secretariat, and then with Thamilselvan, Head of the LTTE political division. Following these meetings, a Peace Secretariat member was asked to take care of me. She took her "walkie" and repeated a word which I could not decipher as Tamil. Later I found that this word was often repeated on the walkies, which were carried by many members. Eventually I learned that this word *saravannai saravannai* was actually Saravanan *annai*. Adding the postfix *annai* to a name means older brother. It is universally used in Tamil culture to refer to someone old enough to be one's older brother.

Saravanan, a wheelchair-bound paraplegic following a war-related injury, was an institution in his own right in Vanni. He operated as the communication hub for the "walkies" owned by LTTE members. Saravanan, a shy man, did his task so admirably, and was respected and loved by all members. During the frequent aerial bombings later on, most LTTE institutions would get an early warning in a coded message on their walkie from Saravanan. He, in turn, somehow received a message whenever a bomber took off in the south. Not surprisingly, his office cum home was the target of Lankan bombers more than once, resulting in the fatalities of his close associates.

Readers may be confused and surprised that I, a mature woman from the Tamil Diaspora, would visit Vanni, a land in the control of a so-called terrorist group, as a relative stranger. It was only during this second trip that I became known to some top LTTE leaders in the political division. However, the Vanni of that time was indeed geared to welcome Tamil Diaspora members. The various LTTE institutions were ready to accommodate such Diaspora visitors. It was, therefore, not unusual for strangers like me to visit Vanni at that time and stay for varying lengths of time and do voluntary work.

In my meeting with Thamilselvan at the Peace Secretariat, I raised what I had just observed at the *makkal thodarpakam* and the need for research into the issue of child soldiers. In fact, the issue of child soldiers in the LTTE was by now a very hot topic, actively followed by foreign diplomats, the Sri Lanka Monitoring Mission (SLMM)—the peace monitors, media, human rights groups, and everyone else. Because of my comment to Thamilselvan, I was given the task of studying the subject. Two immediate outcomes of this project were memorable. Firstly, I had the chance to visit many child-based institutions in Vanni and, secondly, I developed a close working relationship with Karan, an extraordinary individual who assisted me in this and many more future projects I was to be involved in.

Karan had also been a child soldier, and for me, he was like a knowledge tentacle that could reach every nook and corner of LTTE institutions. He was crucial in many documentation projects that I was part of during the four years I spent there. He was my teacher on the history of the armed struggle over the last twenty years or so. He remembered it in great detail. He also knew of documents on many and varied subjects that were scattered around Vanni. When I needed them for my projects, he collected them and gave them to me. His drive to document history, given that he was a child soldier, was amazing. Even in early 2009, he did not give up and was always driving to procure high quality documents. He was killed by shelling in April 2009.

It was with Karan that I first embarked on researching the situation of children affected by the civil war. This first project was to study the child-based programmes instituted to mitigate the effects of war. In other words, the aim was to highlight every aspect, other than the child soldier issue, that had affected children in Vanni. Graca Machel's 1996 global report[2] on children affected by war highlighted several issues. The child soldier issue was one of them. She also identified: unaccompanied internally displaced person (IDP) children, landmine education, health and nutrition, psychological well-being, education, sexual exploitation, and durable solutions. None of these other issues interested most of the people except, of course, the Tamils.

War creates destitute children, and there was no shortage of them in Vanni. There were many homes caring for destitute children. These were deliberately called children's homes and were never referred to as orphanages. With Karan, I first visited half a dozen of these children's homes. Karan collected and collated statistics on children in children's homes throughout the Tamil homeland. He worked out that there were around 6000 children in children's homes. We also obtained the Northeast Provincial Council Statistical book for 2004, and from it worked out there were around 600,000 children under the age of eighteen in the Tamil homeland. Thus, we were able to conclude that one in every one hundred children was being cared for in a children's home. That figure surprised many people. We also worked out, by counting the number of children who had lost both parents in the war, that one in 300 children was in this plight in 2004. Quite a plight the Tamil children were in, even at that time.

During the visits to the children's homes, I recorded what the children said the reasons were for them to be in that institution. Through their narration I could almost discern the entire history of the military attacks and resulting losses and displacements. There were children who told stories about losing parents and siblings in every military attack from the 1980s right until the ceasefire of 2002. The children narrated all forms of attacks on civilians by the Lankan Military that they had directly experienced. The death of parents as a result of bombing and shelling, loss caused by landmines, arrest and disappearance, death due to shooting, and death and injury due to attacks on boats were all in the children's stories. The death of a parent is only one aspect of the trauma faced by the children. Many told stories of how their parents had been injured in the attacks by the Lankan Military and lost their ability to take care of their children. Parents had become separated from their children during displacement, some of them never to be reunited. Perhaps even more difficult for children to comprehend was how their parents could have just walked away from them. Many parents had done so, unable to carry the responsibility under extreme hardship. Some of these parents had come back looking for the children after the ceasefire of 2002. I recorded what the children told me on a tape and transcribed it into English to gather general points for my articles. I would like to reproduce some of what I transcribed below, because their stories paint the situation very well.

Isaiyarasi: She joined the children's home six years earlier. She could remember her mother but not her father. Her father was arrested by the army and had disappeared. Her mother had been in the Kilinochchi hospital due to some illness and died in the aerial bombing of the hospital.

Chanthirika: She was brought up together with her sister by her grandmother. She did not know the whereabouts of her parents, from whom they were separated during the Indian Peace Keeping Force (IPKF) troubles. Her grandmother was also dead at that point. In 2009, just a few weeks before I left Vanni, I met Chanthirika when the vehicle in which I was travelling picked up a few LTTE girls in military attire waiting on the road. Chanthirika was among them, and she asked me with a very broad smile whether I could remember her.

Jeyagowri: She lost both parents in the same shelling incident, in which twelve people died.

Tharshini: After the big Jaffna displacement in 1995, she went to Colombo with her grandmother and uncle. All three of them were arrested by the army, and she spent two years in prison separated from them. When they were released, they came to Vanni. Her grandmother and mother were living together but were too poor to send her to school. Given the devastation caused by the war, one would expect destitute children to roam the streets. This was not the case. I wondered if the LTTE deserved credit for this or whether the Tamil community as a whole and their culture were responsible for these child-centered efforts. One cannot forget that only a couple of decades prior, the following would have been a common scenario in the upper middle class families of this same Tamil community.

"The home belongs to a wealthy family. Two well-groomed children are seated on the floor, playing a game of knucklebones. One of the knucklebones jumps off a child's hand and lands in the yard. The younger of the two children suddenly yells out to someone inside the house, "Ranee, come get the knuckle in the yard." Another child, who looks younger than the one who called out, comes running from the kitchen, where she was washing up some plates, picks up the knucklebone and hands it over and returns back to her work..."

I reflected on scenes which I had witnessed again and again during my younger days in Jaffna, where very young children were used as domestic aids in wealthier families. I was in no doubt that a lot of credit for the care of the children in Vanni must, therefore, go to the LTTE.

TRO, the largest local NGO under LTTE patronage, also ran another type of child center called the "child nutrition park". There were several such nutrition parks caring for hundreds of children at any given time. These parks were set up in areas that were very poor and where both parents needed to go to work for daily wages. These parents tended to leave the very young with older children, effectively harming both; the older child missed schooling and the younger child did not receive adequate care. These nutrition parks took in children between the ages of two and five. Parents could leave them early in the morning on their way to work and pick them up on their way back home. The focus of the nutrition parks was both physical and mental development. Children attended the park six days a week. The children were weighed every month and a record was kept. Medical professionals visited the park regularly and these records gave early warnings of any potential health problems present in the children. Those over the age of four followed a pre-school program. Parents were not charged any fees for this service. However, parents enthusiastically attended all meetings and educational workshops.

The childcare provided in these child institutions, despite poor resources, was very impressive. I was impressed by the dedication of the caregivers.

When these caregivers discussed individual children, they became emotional when talking about the child's background and ecstatic when they listed the child's achievements. A striking feature that was common to these children-centered institutions was the calibre of the people who staffed them. It was not their competence, nor their efficiency, nor their dedication that was striking. It was their total immersion in the work at hand, creating an atmosphere of a tight-knit, family-like unit that was most striking. The cohesion of these family-like units created a nourishing social context in which the staff and beneficiaries were able to enjoy each other while doing what they were there to do. This magnified the effect of the service provided to the beneficiaries far beyond what could be expected for the level of material resource input.

Some of the factors that could have helped to create this culture might be the following. Crisis creates social cohesion among any group of humans, and this was an obvious factor here as well. The type of people who become leaders is dependent on the type of social formation. During times of struggle for justice, it is the more socially-minded people, rather than those who seek power, profit or fame, who will seek roles as leaders. Another factor was the bringing to the fore of a layer of the community that had remained in the bottom stratum of society. South Asian thought patterns, even today, are ridden with caste categorization. Widespread egalitarian thought is foreign to the region. This is what the Western indologist Louis Dumont referred to as the Homo-Hierachicus mode of thinking. The ideologies of the LTTE, which urged the downtrodden to take an active role in the liberation struggle, had challenged this mode of thought. In Vanni, at least within the wider LTTE community, this had created a social context where the old caste and class-based thought processes had been challenged. This new way of conceptualising of society brought a particular calibre of people into leadership roles in the social work organizations. Many of these leaders came from the oppressed communities of the earlier social formation. Members of these communities, being poor and holding onto traditional social interactions, have a way of being that is distinctly different from the modern globalized way of being. They therefore carried this into their social work arena creating a social cohesion that had rarely been seen, previously. It was these social processes that had created the unique culture observable in most social work organizations operating in LTTE-administered areas. This social context would have been worth preserving and nurturing not only for its obvious humanitarian benefits but also as an interesting case study of alternatives to the prevailing Western model of humanitarian work.

I had a rather interesting experience trying to extract words from the international staff working on child rights in Vanni. I asked them about their views on child abuse in children's homes in Vanni. Unlike the scandals that erupted over the World War II children's homes in the West, and even on the rest of the island, there had not been any reports of abuse in the Vanni children's homes. The manner in which these international staff evaded telling me that they had not heard of any reports of abuse gave me an insight. It made me see the straightjacket mandate within which the staff of international agencies were made to work. One international staff member told me that the absence of reports of abuse did not necessarily mean the absence of abuse, which was logically correct. However, their reluctance to speculate on let alone applaud the good record of the children's homes in Vanni was fascinating. At that time international agencies were finding that beating the drums about child soldiers within the LTTE was a rich source for mining funding. Crediting the same group accused of child soldier violation with protecting children from abuse and caring for them surely did not go together. The behaviour of international staff assessing anything related to the LTTE—particularizing the widespread good practices of the LTTE, while generalising whatever bad practice they could observe—was revealing.

Despite the impressive care of at-risk children under the LTTE, after nearly fifteen years of running children's homes, some people in Vanni, I noticed, were becoming aware through firsthand experience of the inadequacy of institutionalizing children perhaps because this was also a constant tune played by child-based international agencies that were working in Vanni. I am sure given the ravages of war, that these children ended up better off cared for in the children's homes rather than in the homes of relatives. It was next to impossible to convince the international agencies that the children's homes under LTTE administration were nothing like the scandalous World War II children's homes of the West.

I believe that LTTE culture ensured that children's homes monitored by them were free of abuse. In the post May 2009, post-LTTE, atmosphere in Vanni, there exist a tendency to proliferate children's homes. It is true that the number of children needing such care has multiplied following the large scale civilian deaths in 2009. But the proliferation of the current kind of children's homes poses a grave danger for paedophilic exploitation, a common crime in the rest of the island and also in other parts of the world.

3

Janani and Senchoolai

My very first visit to Vanni in December 2002, though short, was memorable. On this visit I befriended Janani in the forests of Vallipunam, where the Senchoolai children's home was set up. The location was chosen in order to be as far away from the battle lines of the pre-2002 ceasefire era as possible. I ended up there on the pretext of teaching music on the recorder. Anyone who knows anything about LTTE would have at least heard about the LTTE-run Senchoolai children's home for orphaned girls. This institution was formally opened in 1991 in Jaffna for the increasing number of children orphaned by the civil war.

Janani was one of the legends in LTTE history, known for her association with the Senchoolai children's home from its birth till its end. Janani was close to Mathivathani, Pirapaaharan's wife, because they were taken away together to India from their protest, fasting at Jaffna University in the 1980s. This close association between the two friends continued throughout their involvement in Senchoolai, whose children had the privilege of direct communication with Pirapaaharan and Mathivathani.

Senchoolai in the Vallipunam jungle was truly romantic. Living in scattered mud buildings with thatched roofs, among the native forest trees of *paalai* and *veera*, and animals like monkeys, snakes, plenty of mosquitoes, and even occasional elephants, there were 150 happy girls of all ages, who were superbly cared for. Janani was the *periamma* to all of them and all of them demanded her attention. The word periamma, in this context, conveys affection to someone who fills the role of a mother. I spent three weeks there with a lot of opportunity to discuss various matters with Janani. My friendship with Janani continued right till the end.

In the Vallipunam jungles we planned that I would return and attach myself to Senchoolai. I was excited to have found an institution to attach myself to, because by then I was keen to spend a long time in Vanni. I hardly knew then how futile this plan was, and how I would be distracted first into the North East Secretariat of Human Rights (NESoHR) and later into the LTTE Peace Secretariat. Janani had some grand plan for developing a child development program for war-affected children which emphasized a sense of national pride. As always, her plans were to be carried out first on the Senchoolai children and to be extended later to the wider community. She was completely immersed in Senchoolai, and sometimes appeared to lose sight of the wider world. She would demand all who knew her to also apply ourselves to her grand plans around Senchoolai. Some of them were good, and some of them were very unrealistic, demanding too much of others' time.

I met very young girls as well as older girls. I heard their life stories, the great tragedies they were, in the surrounding Vallipunam jungle. Their stories, from a world very different to mine, sounded even more distant when heard in that surrounding. There was one very smart four-year-old who was rescued from among the ashes of a cemetery, and thus was named Sampavi, deriving from the Tamil word for ashes. There were several older girls who, as very young children, had witnessed the killing of their parents by the Lankan Military in their own home. Some had witnessed large scale massacres. Many of these girls who witnessed gruesome massacres were from the eastern areas, where massacres of civilians were very common in the 1980s, unnoticed by the outside. Many of the girls had brothers in Senchoolai's brother institution, Arivuchchoolai.

In the Vallipunam jungle, the girls had a computer building where they had access to four or five desktop computers. The mud buildings, around fifteen of them, were spread over a sprawling area, and at night, without light, walking from one hut to another when snakes could be slithering on the ground could be a bit creepy. But the girls walked without any light and with ease. When I pointed out to one older girl that this was risky and we should carry a torch light, she responded,

"We have lived like this for many years without any of us ever being bitten by a snake. We leave the snakes alone and they leave us alone."

That seemed like very profound knowledge on living with nature.

Janani was already planning to shift Senchoolai to Kilinochchi so that the girls would have better access to education and other opportunities. This of course entailed gaining access to a large land area, which was the main issue she was dealing with at that time.

It was typical for LTTE institutions to have someone be responsible for giving a tumbler of tea to visitors. In the early days of the 2002 ceasefire, just recovering from a devastating war phase, all the institutions were only mud huts sprawling over large pieces of land. One small hut would be the tea house and would be separate from the kitchen, which not all institutions would have. A pot of water would be always at near boiling point on an open fire in the tea house. The tea-person would bring tumblers of tea to visitors within a few minutes of their arrival.

At Senchoolai, a few times, I had tea inside the tea house, sitting on the mud floor and chatting to the tea-person. Sometimes other members of Senchoolai would drop in, and the conversation that followed would be warm and unique, and one that could take place only in such settings of very egalitarian and highly interdependent community living.

Unlike all other children's homes in Vanni, Senchoolai for girls and Arivuchchoolai for boys were funded directly by LTTE and were staffed by many LTTE members. In the case of Senchoolai, it was female members under Janani's leadership. Only a few LTTE members holding positions of high responsibility in these two institutions were permanently attached to them. Other members might have been assigned to these two institutions for period of time, and later moved out. All LTTE members, not just those serving in these two institutions, were encouraged to develop a special, caring relationship toward these two children's home. Most LTTE members did have a special place in their heart for these two institutions that was different from the way they related to other children's homes.

In Senchoolai, functioning in the Vallipunam jungles, I met three or four very junior LTTE members, some of whom may have been under the age of eighteen, clearly younger than the older girls of Senchoolai. Two of these girls were assigned to look after me, and I met them several times a day when they brought food and tea. They were always smiling and said their age was eighteen. I was not completely at ease about these young LTTE members because they seemed naive and not the picture of a typical freedom fighter one imagines. Yet, I could see that they were happy because of the camaraderie they had.

I did not ask them why they joined LTTE because I already knew their answer: "*To fight for our country.*" I was not inclined to interrogate them further at that time, and in fact I never asked any LTTE member why they joined the movement because their answer to this would have been typical, as many Diaspora Tamils who asked this question found out. Later in 2007, I did ask a few female members whom I had come to know well this question, in order to write a document about it. I found out an interesting array of answers which are described later in the book.

Janani had instinctively decided that children must be provided with an environment as close to a home as possible to give them stability. Thus, Senchoolai was made up of many homes, with an adult employee under whose care were around 10—15 girls. The LTTE members attached to Senchoolai were not in charge of any particular home, but had overall responsibilities in different areas like education, health, clothing, food, office administration, building and yard maintenance etc. The biggest challenge for Janani was not finding the funding needed to do this, because Pirapaaharan was always ready to channel funds to Senchoolai. The problem was to find good people willing to do this job for a standard salary in the area. It went against the norms of society to expect an older woman to be a live-in worker, away from her own family. Most of the people who ended up being employed at Senchoolai were also those affected by the war and thus had lost their family units. After the 2002 ceasefire, there were not many people who were looking to live and work there, abandoning their own families, but there were some, and Senchoolai did well despite this problem.

It was from one of these older woman carers that I learnt the true Vanni concept of the Tamil word *poorali* while we discussed her family. It was not that she explained it to me, but her mannerism and body language when she used that phrase that conveyed the special status a *poorali* had in the hearts of the people. Understanding it then crystallized in my mind something about the Vanni society that had been gradually forming. I would go as far as to say that most societies that are waging a struggle that demanded a great deal of sacrifice from its fighters would have similar conceptions.

I cannot leave out another highlight at Senchoolai in the Vallipunam jungles—the monkeys. They were everywhere. Suddenly they would descend as a troupe and walk around on the ground, on the fence, on the roof, and climb the trees among the huts. Once when we were there, an eight-year-old girl could not resist picking up a tiny baby monkey which was lagging behind. The mother grabbed the girl's feet and ran as the girl also tried to run. It let go of the girl only when she put the baby monkey down. It was fascinating to watch the mother's attempt to reclaim her baby without actually attacking the girl—almost as if it too knew that these were special girls who should not be harmed. An older girl later told me how the monkeys would enter their huts—none of which had lockable doors—and unzip their bags and take things away.

Talking of monkeys and children in the children's home, another scene I observed in another children's home, Kurukulam, where I stayed for two weeks, is worth recording. This institution was located in Kilinochchi on land that had been used by humans for many decades; thus, it had several mature mango trees that provided soothing shade. My visit was during mango season when the mangoes on the trees were so very inviting for the children. However, for safety reasons the children were not permitted to climb the trees or throw stones at the fruit to bring it down. The children had worked out a much more interesting way of bringing the fruit down. When the fruit were in season, monkeys regularly visited in packs to feast on it. All the children had to do was stand under the trees, look up at the monkeys, make some noises, and jump up and down. The monkeys would do the same on the tree branches, bringing the near-ripe mangoes down!

The girls and adults in Senchoolai suffered repeated malaria attacks, although they were regularly given preventive medication. The girls' description of the malaria medication sounded worse than the malaria itself. Later on, in 2006, I was pleasantly surprised to learn that the LTTE health division, together with the Lankan health sector in Vanni, had completely eradicated malaria. It was an astounding achievement that highlighted the LTTE's capacities and the concern for the well being of the people. I was told that the delay in achieving this success was purely due to the pre-2002 embargo placed by the Lankan government on anti-malarial spray reaching Vanni. Indeed, health sector professionals in Vanni repeatedly raised the alarm of a repeat malarial outbreak when this embargo on malarial spray was re-imposed in 2007.

When we left the Senchoolai in 2002, Janani was in the sickbay hut suffering a bout of malaria. I met Janani again in 2004 during my second visit and strengthened our friendship. Half of Senchoolai had by now shifted to a temporary building in Kilinochchi which was very near the Tank Hotel in front of the Kanagambikai Lake, where I stayed during my second visit of three months duration. Most of my time during this trip was filled with boredom—stuck in my room at the Tank Hotel because unless one had one's own transport, it was difficult to get anywhere in Vanni. However, the temporary abode of Senchoolai in Kilinochchi, located near the Tank Hotel, filled my time pleasantly. In the middle of this Senchoolai land, shaded by a canopy of mango trees, there was a large open shed. It was cool and breezy and I could just sit there and watch the girls do whatever they did. No one questioned why I was there because I was Janani's friend.

This Kilinochchi land, on which Senchoolai was located, was deemed unsuitable for a children's home with dense habitation because the underground water level rose too high and was unsuitable for toilet pits. Thus, Janani was still on the lookout for other land for Senchoolai's permanent abode. As a result, the facilities available there were very minimal and the staff and the girls struggled to maintain it.

It was at this time that Janani gave me the responsibility of writing the history of Senchoolai, and to this end I had the privilege of holding long discussions with one other senior LTTE member attached to Senchoolai. Janani did not give me the freedom to write the history in my style. This being one of my early assignments in Vanni, I was also reluctant to exert my own style. This limitation resulted in me writing a brief history, which was effectively Janani's history of Senchoolai. My contribution to it, except to put words on paper, was to clean up the statistics on the children who were cared for at Senchoolai, digitize it, and produce a few graphs based on it. As far as I can tell, this written history was lost during 2009 along with every other document in Vanni that was not uploaded to the internet. For this reason, and as a tribute to Janani, who had such passion for Senchoolai's history, I should dwell on this project a little more.

Based on my recollection, about 450 children had been through Senchoolai and around 200 of them were still attached to it. Initially Senchoolai took in boys and girls, but as the boys grew up a separate home, Arivuchchoolai, was set up for them. An aspect of Senchoolai history that Janani was never tired of emphasizing was the repeated displacement it faced. When I wrote the history, it had already been displaced sixteen or seventeen times. It is not hard to imagine the effect that would have had on the children.

Some, perhaps about 150 of them, officially left Senchoolai because a member of their family managed to trace them. Quite a few left in such a manner after 2002. Some unsettled ones ran away and as a result ended up in the gutters. Janani never lost touch with the girls who had married and physically left the Senchoolai abode. The connection was always maintained and the girls returned with their husbands and children to visit regularly. A constant problem faced by Senchoolai was the persistent attempt by some of the girls to run away to join the LTTE. They would use all kinds of lies to hide from LTTE recruiters where they were from, because the LTTE had a strict policy of not recruiting anyone from the children's homes. One LTTE member from Senchoolai told me about the endless struggle she went through and the enormous time she had spent retrieving the girls who had run away to join the LTTE by lying about their association with Senchoolai. Some of those who showed great determination by repeatedly running away were allowed to remain in the LTTE, but they visited Senchoolai regularly. There were around fifteen girls from Senchoolai who were official LTTE members and another ten who were *maaveerar* by this time.

Janani also ensured that all the girls at Senchoolai were trained in a vocation that could earn them a living. There were police-women, lawyers, medics, nurses, school teachers, seamstresses, cooks, typists. You name it, they had them. In fact since its inception, Senchoolai ran its own school. It thrived when Senchoolai was functioning in Jaffna because it had the support of many of Jaffna's educators at that time. With the mass displacement of 1995, the support continued. As many of the educationalists drifted back to Jaffna, Senchoolai School lost a lot of such support. Eventually, there was a push from LTTE to close the school and send the girls to the mainstream schools. Janani fought hard against this, using the performance statistics of the girls at GCE-O/L to show that they performed better if they attended the Senchoolai School. She recruited many people, including me, to support her case. Senchoolai eventually found an excellent new permanent abode in Kilinochchi, and with it Janani also lost her case for a Senchoolai School entirely under her management.

Almost all the older girls I met in the Vallipunam jungle residence were married with children by the time of the 2008 Kilinochchi evacuation. I believe there were close to fifty of them. The vast majority of them married LTTE members, either by arrangement or by finding their own partner. Most of them appeared to be happily married with the girls taking the traditional wifely role in the partnership. Their husbands were more considerate than an average Tamil man due to the LTTE culture of respect for women.

Many of the girls who came to Senchoolai as school-aged children had missed many years of school. One senior LTTE member within Senchoolai told me that at first many of the girls did not even have decent hygiene habits, and they had to struggle to teach them everything from how to use the toilet and sanitary pads to how to take a bath using soap, etc. These same girls, three or four years later, learned to read and write. Some of the intelligent ones even sat and passed GCE-O/L examinations. The struggle and dedication of LTTE members to make these dysfunctional girls into functional people, who later married decent LTTE men to lead happy married lives, are among the heart-warming stories that have hardly been told. That is because LTTE did not want, in order to claim credit for this achievement, to underline the fact that some of them came to Senchoolai as dysfunctional girls. Senchoolai girls were afforded a high reputation in Vanni, and LTTE did not want that reputation to be diluted in any way.

It must come as no surprise that Janani and Senchoolai had their share of heartaches, given the environment in which they were trying to achieve something. While LTTE poured funds into Senchoolai and also Arivuchchoolai, I suspect Senchoolai was a very special project for Pirapaaharan because it was to do with girls. It is my guess, based on what I have heard said about him by feminist-leaning female LTTE members, that he understood the importance of offering an equal place in society to girls. Given that Senchoolai had such a pride of place within LTTE, and received special treatment in terms of funding, there was also high expectation that the Senchoolai girls would shine academically. In this respect, Senchoolai was a great disappointment to the entire LTTE. Janani had a constant struggle on her hands to convince the LTTE hierarchy that what Senchoolai girls had achieved was indeed outstanding, though not in terms of academic performance. Janani was losing her battle in this regard, and she was deeply hurt by it.

The girls at Senchoolai who had joined as school-aged children had undergone traumatic experiences, and those who had joined as babies lacked adequate parental sustenance despite all the efforts within Senchoolai. Both types went through a turbulent adolescent period and many lost direction and drive. Though most recovered due to the support given, this phase left its mark on their academic performance. Thus Janani had to face the criticism for Senchoolai's lack of academic excellence.

During 2005, Janani spoke often of needing a holiday. I was taken aback that her idea of a holiday was doing sentry post duty alone in a jungle area with a gun and book. She never got to do it.

Janani developed her vision for Senchoolai over a period of time, and, following the 2002 ceasefire, she began a drive to document the history and also her vision. She wrote a brief document consisting of a few pages, with each page outlining her vision of different aspects of Senchoolai. I have forgotten what she wrote in it, but remember it as a good document. One of the things that I remember, and it is also one topic she repeated many times, was her insight on the need to eradicate from Tamil society the word "orphan" and all the connotations that go with it of a diminished and second-class child. Within Vanni, the LTTE and Janani together achieved it through the work of Senchoolai. Janani would insist on claiming this credit entirely for Senchoolai. She asked me for a title for the brief document she wrote, and the title, "Senchoolai—a concept", seemed very apt.

One of the negative aspects of Senchoolai that I met with in my own line of work on child soldiers was Janani's desire to keep Senchoolai far too closely associated with the LTTE. Over and above her membership cum politico-military association with LTTE, Janani, like many LTTE members, had an emotional connection with Pirapaaharan. I noticed that for female members there was another dimension to this emotional connection—one of a protector who gave them respect and freedom in a male-dominated world. For Janani, this emotional connection went further due to their closeness, and she treated Pirapaaharan like her older brother who cared a lot about his sister. The sister-brother relationship in Tamil culture has been the subject of anthropological exploration, and this aspect dominated Janani's relationship with Pirapaaharan.

It was because of this emotional link that she failed to appreciate the value of distancing Senchoolai from the LTTE. Walking into Senchoolai, one noticed the paraphernalia was all about the LTTE. LTTE members walked in and out of Senchoolai in their full military gear. Because of this culture, organizations like UNICEF were not allowed easy access to Senchoolai, fuelling speculation that Senchoolai was a breeding ground for Tiger cubs. This certainly did not help the prevailing LTTE image of child recruiter—more on that later when I describe my experiences in working with the LTTE to release child soldiers.

Sometime in 2006, Senchoolai and Arivuchchoolai found their permanent abode, which was an excellent set of buildings and facilities. In July 2006, Senchoolai celebrated its anniversary in its new location. A lot of documentation on Senchoolai that had been written was officially published at this function. To my knowledge this documentation included: a review by an educationalist of Senchoolai's educational achievement, the Senchoolai vision document produced by Janani, the brief history that I wrote in English which was translated into Tamil by Yogi Yogaratnam, a book by a Senchoolai girl about her experiences, and an anniversary souvenir with many articles on Senchoolai. I am not sure if any copies of these publications have survived.

Until the shift in 2006 to their permanent abodes, the two institutions, Senchoolai for girls and Arivuchchoolai for boys, were located further apart. Their new abodes in 2006 were located right next to each other. I visited Arivuchchoolai on a few occasions. My first visit was in 2004 during my study tour of children's homes. I also visited a few more times during my work on child soldiers. Though my involvement with Arivuchchoolai was not as extensive as my involvement with Senchoolai, as far as I could see they both functioned along similar lines. In fact, a few more boys from Arivuchchoolai were attending Jaffna University at this time compared to students from Senchoolai.

Sometime in 2007, Janani attempted to draw me into the Senchoolai circle again. Having achieved the residential needs, and even their educational needs to some extent, Janani had started to think about the psychological health of the girls. She wanted me to be involved though I had no training in this field. I read a lot and decided that I could contribute by encouraging and helping all the girls to develop a folder on the theme "Who am I?" I put some thought into it and described my ideas to Janani. Janani dismissed my ideas, suggesting that such an exercise could upset the girls, and with that I dropped the idea.

The very last project in which Janani tried to include me was in mid-2008. She described the project's aim and said it was to create a document that could be used as a guide by everyone involved in running children's homes. This was a worthy project, but it evolved into a document that concentrated only on Senchoolai, which was atypical of all the children's homes in Vanni. The other children's homes did not have the same level resources that were available to Senchoolai which cared for orphaned children with no dependable extended family to care about them. Whereas the children in the other children's homes were poverty stricken but had contact with some family member. She invited about twelve Tamil civilians in Vanni working in journalism, IT, teaching, NGOs, etc., to team up in groups of two to tackle different aspects of Senchoolai's growth.

The late journalist Sathiamoorthy was asked by Janani to work with me on the project covering the area of education. I was grateful for the opportunity to work closely with Sathiamoorthy as he wrote down his perception of Senchoolai in the area of education. Sathiamoorthy, a humble man, was well known among the Tamil Diaspora for his part in the TTN television service provided by the international wing of the LTTE, where he regularly presented excellent political analysis. Through the Senchoolai project, I learnt of his writing ability too. If he had survived May 2009, we would have a brilliant recording by him about Vanni at that time. I could not attend most of the meetings related to this Senchoolai project, but I had lengthy discussions with Sathiamoorthy about it. All of us were displaced from Kilinochchi in October 2008. I last saw Sathiamoorthy on the Tharmapuram road with his wife, pushing his bicycle loaded with World Food Programme (WFP) food rations. He gave me a wave and his usual polite smile, and appeared to be taking the ordeal of displacement in stride, despite having a two-year-old daughter whom he adored. Sathiamoorthy was killed in Lankan shelling in February 2009. This last Senchoolai project in which I was involved never materialized.

Following the displacement from Kilinochchi, I was living in another children's home, Senthalir, in Vallipunam, run by the Centre for Women's Development and Rehabilitation (CWDR). While staying there in early 2009, I heard that the older residents of Senchoolai and Arivuchchoolai were being made to join the LTTE's military effort to fend off the Lankan Military. I do not know if it was only those over the age of eighteen who were made to go to frontline duty. I never met Janani after the Kilinochchi evacuation. Some LTTE members tell me that she refused to walk out of the war zone and remained inside. She most likely took her own life or she may have been killed.

I have no firsthand information about what has happened to the children from Senchoolai, many of whom I came to know well. There were news reports that at least some were being cared for in children's homes in Vavuniya. There was one media report on the death of one Senchoolai girl, Shalini, in a Vavuniya institution. During my attempts to re-establish links with Senchoolai in 2007, I talked to some of the older girls about the internet and said that I could bring them information on a topic that interested them. It was Shalini who showed the most interest, and she requested information about galaxies and the solar system. She was an intelligent, thoughtful, and sensitive girl.

4

Rituals

The three-week stay with Janani at Senchoolai during my first trip towards the end of 2002, and visits with Karan to the children's home during my second trip in 2004, were the highlights of my Vanni experience to this point. My in-depth four-year Vanni experience only began during my third trip in early 2005. Before delving into my four years there, I want to describe the pervasive rituals in Vanni at that time. Many aspects of these rituals were rather unique and also visible to most visitors. All of these were destroyed, together with the rest of Vanni, in the final war in 2009.

Religious rituals in Vanni remained just that, and these rituals were the domain of the traditional authorities to manage. But another set of events in the political-community domain was controlled and managed by the LTTE. These gatherings and associated rituals pervaded life in Vanni. The events after the 2002 ceasefire were probably a lot more grandiose than what they would have been like during the earlier war-phase. There were memorial days for individual *maaveerar*; anniversary days for local institutions; opening ceremonies for new institutions as well as new buildings for old institutions; and many special events on a grand scale like *Maaveerar thinam, Karumpuli thinam, and Ponkuthamil. Thaiponkal,* a traditional Tamil festival, was also grandly celebrated by the LTTE. Then there were street dramas and musical events as well as stage performances. There were also frequent protest marches against the actions of the Lankan government. The list goes on. The visits of Western representatives with their large entourages of media personnel were also conducted in a very ritualistic style, without real political substance, both by the LTTE and the visitors. This I describe later.

Something equivalent to shrines were permanently installed in most LTTE offices. In other places, like schools and government offices, they were set up temporarily on the ritual days. The permanent shrines would include pictures of the *maaveerar* who were from that division. Most such shrines would have had about twenty pictures. These shrines were revered. One was constantly reminded of the ultimate sacrifice of the fallen as one paid respect by lighting the lamp and offering flowers. Most LTTE institutions endeavored to start the working day by spending a few minutes at the shrine. Indeed, many of the rituals of the LTTE were aimed at keeping the memories of the *maaveerar* alive in the minds of the people.

There was one icon that also received tribute. This was an upright gun with a military hat draped on the top of its barrel. The whole thing stood on a small rocky mount about a meter in diameter and a meter high. There are multiple sources for this reverence for the gun. It is a way of paying tribute to the armed struggle, emphasizing the "armed" part. It also derives from cultures, such as the Tamil culture, where it is common to pay tribute to the tools of one's livelihood. For example, carpenters, blacksmiths, farmers, etc., practice placing their tools of trade in front of the local gods and pay tribute. In the case of the gun on the mount, the god part is removed, but one still offers flowers and lights the lamp; mentally offering a high degree of respect to it.

There were also open-air shrines which were installed with pictures of fallen heroes. These received the same reverence as an icon in a shrine. There were also statues of those who were well-known among the fallen erected at some street junctions. Everyone who drove on the A9 road through Kilinochchi would have noticed statues and pictures of the fallen, and the gun draped with a hat erected on major intersections. A reputed Tamilnaadu sculptor stayed in Kilinochchi for an extended period of time, teaching students the art of sculpture and also creating statues for installation. I had the privilege of observing him at work. In fact, many reputed artists, in varying fields like art and filmmaking, from Tamilnaadu visited Kilinochchi during this period and conducted classes for the locals.

The icons of the armed struggle were ubiquitous in all parts of daily life. Later on, as the signs of war intensified, these icons were further complemented with large billboards on the road highlighting the atrocities of the Lankan army and calling on the young to join the armed struggle. One billboard had a picture of a young woman pointing a gun, and the words asking the young men whether they were going to let her do the fighting while they gathered at roadsides to gossip.

On the special ritual days, people in most institutions in Vanni, both LTTE and civilian, would gather at their respective shrines for a longer than usual ritual. At a specified time, around nine o'clock in the morning, just prior to the start of the working day, the flag anthem would be broadcast on the Voice of Tigers radio station. An important person from that institution would then raise the LTTE flag. In LTTE institutions it would be always an LTTE member who would raise the flag. In public institutions, such as educational centers and Lankan government offices, the civilian head of that institution would raise the flag. A two-minute silence was observed after the flag hoisting. This ritual silence has now become part of almost all the gatherings of people of Tamil Eelam origin spread across the world. Institutions of international agencies in Vanni did not take part in these rituals, though they had to respect the practice.

Most LTTE members at the gathering would give their traditional salute during the flag rising by placing their opened right hand in the middle of their chest. Rarely civilians did this, though there were occasional exceptions. This was therefore a reliable way to identify members who were in civilian clothes. If the shrine included the gun and hat icon, after the flag hoisting respect was paid to it first by garlanding it, and only then, the pictures of individual *maaveerar* were respected by lighting the lamp and offering flowers. These rituals were usually short, lasting less than thirty minutes. There would be a short talk during these rituals, and often this took most of the ritual time with people generally paying little attention to it. Everyone was encouraged to attend these rituals. Notable ritual days included *Maaveerar thinam* which ran over three days, *Thileepan thinam* which ran over twelve days, *Karumpuli thinam, Annai Poopathi thinam, Penkal ezuchchi thinam,* and *Col. Kiddu thinam.*

The day of the *Maaveerar thinam* on 27 November is a day unlike any other. The entire society enters into a different mood. For the whole week prior to this day, the streets would gain a festive atmosphere, with all kinds of decorations and scores of installations in memory of *maaveerar.* On this day, families of *maaveerar* would have started to visit the many *thuyilum-illam* from the morning. The old and the less able people would visit the *thuyilum-illam* during the day, because during the evening climax these places were packed with people. I met such older folk visiting the *thuyilum-illam* earlier during *Maaveerar thinam.* Their attitude and their state of mind towards this ritual were unique and blurred the boundaries between paying a visit to a loved one and visiting a temple on a special day. The evening event was undoubtedly one of a kind in the whole world.

Flower garlands for the graves were an essential part of visiting the graves on this day. The demand for flowers on this day was so huge that flowers became a rare commodity. People would decorate the graves with flowers and fruits, and light incense. They would stand around the graves of their family member; wailing as if the family member had just left them. One can imagine this scene repeated many thousands of times in front of the many thousands of graves in a *thuyilum-illam.* That was the climax of Maaveerar Day. It was difficult not to be moved by it.

The LTTE Peace Secretariat had an open-air shrine near it that belonged to the political headquarters nearby. I attended the rituals there on many occasions. It would mostly be Thamilselvan who would raise the flag. Rituals are a valuable practice to maintain cohesion among a large group of people. They are employed in most human endeavors, ranging from secular cultural practices to religious practices to political parties to military groups. Yet, some very loyal LTTE members expressed to me their disdain over these rituals, especially the flag anthem. I could see a parallel between these loyal LTTE members who nevertheless expressed disdain for LTTE rituals and deeply religious people who nevertheless desist from taking part in ritualistic religious practices.

There were other events that were also grandiose. *Ponkuthamil* was one of them. During 2004—2005 these events were staged in all the main centers in Tamil Eelam, like a serialized show. There were also reports of harassment of the Tamils travelling to attend these shows by the Lankan Military. I attended one massive *Ponkuthamil* event in Kilinochchi that was attended by more than 10,000 people. The people were singing and chanting in unison. Some chants called on the "international community" to listen to the voice of the people. I, for the first time in my life, heard such freedom chants by a massive crowd. It was quite emotional because it highlighted the neglect and apathy of the international community to the plight of the ordinary Tamil people and their appeal for freedom. These shows clearly demonstrated to the international community that was brokering the peace process the level of support among the people for an independent Tamil Eelam. The shows also indirectly created awareness among the Tamils of the tardiness of the international conduct of the peace process.

This *Ponkuthamil* event took place during the no-war-no-peace time of early 2005. It was a period when even minor events in Vanni were enthusiastically reported by the international media, due to the ongoing peace process. I was astounded that the international media did not carry any news items about this massive gathering. The media did not consider such a massive gathering of the Vanni public, calling for the attention of the peace-brokers, worthy of reporting. Students of the international media would find this example worthy of further investigation.

There were frequent civilian-based protests against many Lankan actions, which were clearly organized by the LTTE. Due to the LTTE control of civilian protests, they failed to exhibit the show of spontaneity that one would expect in such civilian-based protests. They were executed with military-like precision and thus failed to inspire and convince others watching the protest. This, however, did not mean that the civilians were not identifying with the causes behind the protests; rather, by being denied control of their protests, they lacked the spirit one usually expects in such protests.

There were also frequent musical road shows. These were based on *therukkooththu*, an ancient local folk art form, a kind of music-drama for the enjoyment of the rich and the poor. In earlier days, they were mainly used to tell religious stories and sometimes the stories of ancient kings. This art form was now used in Vanni to convey themes of politics, war, and struggle. They were of a very high standard, with humor, political satire, and an important political message. They were very enjoyable indeed. The old art form of *therukkooththu,* now conveying the new political messages, was freely available to the bottom stratum of the society. In its message and in its free availability this may have been a first of its kind for the people of Tamil Eelam, and perhaps the only one to date.

Government hospitals destroyed by bombing prior to 2002 were rebuilt with international aid. There were buildings galore funded by international aid and Diaspora funds. Schools and the many children's homes had new buildings. Destroyed temples and churches were also rebuilt. There was always a new institution or a new building for an old institution being opened, and each one would be a marked by a ceremony of sorts. Many institutions, like the children's homes, celebrated their annual day with invitations to notable personalities. All of these ceremonies would have the flag raising part, but not all of them would have the remainder of the above-mentioned rituals. These ceremonies, as well as the ritual days, provided opportunities for the young artists to perform on stage using nationalist songs. There were a handful of senior members who were most sought after as speakers in such events, such as Balakumar and Ilankumaran alias Baby Subramanium. Both of them have disappeared following capture by the Lankan Military as they walked out of the war zone during the end war in 2009.

Thaiponkal was deliberately made into a national festival because it was non-religious. More importantly, it was the only ancient Tamil festival that had survived. All other traditional festivals celebrated by Tamils are religious and are mixed up with Sanskritic Hinduism or colonial Christianity. *Thaiponkal* was also the festival of the farmers, and Vanni was very much a farming community. On *Thaiponkal* day, a large area in Kilinochchi on the A9 road was a center of the celebration, where *ponkal* (sweet rice pudding) was cooked in one hundred pots in open fire surrounded by grand decorations.

During special days senior LTTE members visited the many welfare institutions. On one particular *Thaiponkal* day I was asked to be at some of the institutions, and Thamilselvan, too, was on a visiting round that day. Our paths crossed at Anpuchchoolai old people's home and at Mayoori-illam, a home for wheelchair-bound, battle-scarred female LTTE members. At Mayoori-illam, the *Thaiponkal* occasion when Thamilselvan and I met, was very warm and informal. While we all waited for the *ponkal* to finish cooking, the resident LTTE members joked freely with Thamilselvan. Another senior LTTE member, who accompanied Thamilselvan, entertained everyone with his beautiful voice. At Anpuchchoolai, Thamilselvan handed out presents to the old people, and I too received the same. He made sure I was not offended by being given the same presents as those that were given to the old people. I thought then that I certainly would not mind staying at this old people's home for the rest of my life. The staff had a very warm and jovial relationship with the old people. The temperate climate and the vast spaces with large shady trees gave the place a very romantic atmosphere. It was very pleasant indeed.

5

NESoHR's clients

My four-year-long involvement with Vanni began with my role as the secretary of North East Secretariat on Human Rights (NESoHR). Indeed, the very first ceremony I attended in Vanni was the opening of NESoHR in July 2004. Only the night before, I was roped into becoming its secretary by its chairperson, Father M. X. Karunaradnam. I did not actually get to work at NESoHR until a few months later in early 2005 because I had to leave Vanni during the intervening period. From March 2005, I worked full time at NESoHR for over a year. After about one year, I left NESoHR in order to be involved with the LTTE Peace Secretariat. NESoHR Chairperson Fr. Karunaradnam was assassinated in April 2008 in Mallavi inside Vanni by a Lankan anti-personnel claymore mine. Following his assassination, I returned to work in NESoHR until it stopped functioning in January 2009.

The creation of NESoHR was the result of two independent processes. Prior to the ceasefire, in the absence of any independent authority to deal with complaints by civilians against the Lankan Military and LTTE, voluntary bodies, called "citizens' committees", were formed to listen to people's complaints. Such citizens' committees had existed throughout the war period in many parts of Tamil Eelam. Also, the international peace-brokers of the 2002 ceasefire were keen on creating a human rights body to function in Vanni. The LTTE initially planned for such a body to function within the LTTE Peace Secretariat, which in turn was created to support the Norwegian-brokered 2002 ceasefire. But some leading members of citizens' committees in Jaffna, Kilinochchi, Trincomalee, and Batticaloa, led by Fr. Karunaradnam, got together and put pressure on the LTTE to create a civilian human rights body. NESoHR was the outcome of these two independent processes, and as such NESoHR retained a level of independence from the LTTE.

Fr. Karunaradnam was popularly called Kili-father. Because he was a Catholic priest, the spirit of caring for the down trodden was reflected within NESoHR. The building itself was a renovated old building that was used by the local cooperative society. It had a crack running down one of the walls, which had been plastered over. Though the layout was not great, the hospitality extended had genuine warmth. People came with complaints not only from all over Vanni but were also from Jaffna and even Trincomalee. The vast majority of cases handled by NESoHR in those early days, however, were to do with the release of LTTE members from the LTTE itself, and not necessarily all of them because they were under the age of eighteen. These were early days for me in Vanni, and I kept away from dealing with complaints against the LTTE—Kili-father was the authority in this. It was interesting to observe the proceedings, though.

Often mothers brought complaints where they wanted their son or daughter over the age of eighteen to be released because that child happened to be their only remaining child able to look after them in their old age. Sometimes Kili-father was able to bring about the child's release. Seeing the parents paying homage and their gratitude towards Kili-father warmed everyone in the office. There was one 21-year-old member released this way in early 2005. She was the only daughter of a destitute mother. The girl obviously had been in the movement for a few years—you could tell. There was no way such a destitute mother in the war zone could have brought up such a smart and confident young woman. The young woman, who had a bubbly personality, commented as she walked away that she would be back in the LTTE fold in no time. The mother was heard retorting back, *"How would you know about my troubles, the endless walks to offices to get your release?"* To which the young woman only had laughter as answer.

While there were many cases where the released young person was happy to be released, most of these had joined the LTTE recently, influenced by LTTE propaganda and later became disillusioned because of the strenuous training regime. However, in those early days following the 2002 ceasefire, this was not the majority. In fact, I saw this family-young person-LTTE triangular tug-a-war being played out innumerable times. The young persons who got caught in the triangular tug-of-war often came from families with problematic backgrounds. In Vanni, under conditions of war and oppression spanning three decades, there was no shortage of families with problematic backgrounds.

I and others viewed Kili-father's ability to resolve complaints against the LTTE with awe. Kili-father had a very special and longstanding relationship with Thamilselvan. It was based on shared trauma during the past phases of the war. It appeared to me at that time that the resolution of complaints against the LTTE depended on this special relationship. Kili-father would take the complaints that were resistant to resolution to Thamilselvan. It appeared that someone in authority within the LTTE had decided that a particular complaint, such as releasing an underage person, need not be effected. It then became necessary for direct influence from Thamilselvan to effect the change, which Kili-father was able to bring about.

Kili-father was also an ardent environmentalist and would not hesitate to take on anyone whom he saw as disrespecting or destroying the precious environment. He was in love with the sea and its resources, and he could speak endlessly about it. He thoroughly enjoyed nature—the seas and the forests. He was against the Sethusamuththiram project planned by India to deepen the narrow sea between India and the Sri Lanka to allow large ships to navigate through it. He feared that this will destroy the rich underwater ecology of the area. His passion for protecting the environment sprang from a deep understanding of nature and how humans had lived in cooperation with it for millennia. He talked about the dying practices within the Tamil culture, such as the habits of farming, fishing, and food preparation that had sustained rather than depleted nature.

His residence in Maankulam in Vanni was a garden paradise. It was like a miniature botanical garden with many exotic plants. He would take visitors through it, showing off his plants like a proud mother. He had a pair of deer, rather large specimens, which were taller than him. They would welcome him on sight and stretch out their necks so Kili-father could kiss them on their faces. He would embrace them and talk to them like he was talking to humans. He never wore any footwear even when walking on rough ground, as a sign of respect to mother earth.

Once, I was in his car with a few other people, and we were driving from Jaffna to Kilinochchi, prior to the closure of the A9 road in mid-2006. He blocked the UN vehicle that was behind and wanting to pass us. He made his efforts in doing so a metaphor for the struggle against the UN in general, which was widely seen within the Tamil community as oppressing the Tamils. Everyone in the car enjoyed it. To my disappointment, Kili-father liked ceremonies to be grand. He spared no expense in celebrating the December 10th Human Rights Day as a political statement to the outsiders.

The second most common complaint brought to NESoHR during those early days following the 2002 ceasefire were land-related matters. The legal status of many plots of land occupied by the people was uncertain at this stage. The complaints related to land that were brought to NESoHR often involved a civilian and an LTTE member. People hoped for some recourse at NESoHR, though land matters should not have fallen under the purview of NESoHR. Kili-father also had difficulty in changing his hat from that of a priest serving his parish to that of the head of a human rights institution. Indeed at NESoHR, even some marriage-related conflicts were handled by Kili-father, prompting a former chief justice of Norway, Carsten Smith, who visited NESoHR in 2005, to comment that NESoHR has become an all-in-one center for helping people. I found this overwhelming and in my opinion went against the grain for structure in a work place.

I later learned that this lack of structure within NESoHR, and Kili-father's efforts to convert NESoHR into an all-in-one center, had also upset the Police Head of that time, Nadeesan. After he had become the Head of the political division, Nadeesan told me that Kili-father tried to take on the role of the courts in dealing with land related conflicts. I believe this puts the situation in context: one is driven to help the downtrodden by using whatever power he can garner, and the other is trying to protect his turf and maintain structure. I think this disagreement between the two men also led to Kili-father being denied the freedom of access to the prisons that he demanded.

People did bring some complaints against the Police Force of the LTTE, though there were not many in those early days of the 2002 ceasefire. One particular case I recall reveals the state of affairs at that time. This complaint related to a bullock cart race, a popular traditional sport. There was some disagreement between the rival sides about the race outcome, and this had led to some clashes. The police stepped in. The complaint was brought to NESoHR by the mother of one of those arrested following the clashes. She was denied access to her arrested son in prison, and she also complained of ill treatment of her son.

For someone like me, who until then had learned about the LTTE mostly by reading and a bit of listening to other Tamils, seeing NESoHR at closer quarters was a huge learning experience. It was a meeting point of Tamil civilians and LTTE, a new form of *makkal thodarpakam* under the watchful eyes of Kili-father. In due course, the number of cases brought to NESoHR on land conflicts waned, and the second most common complaint became those against LTTE actions against people who evaded its taxation. Taxation-related complaints had to do with goods brought in by trucks on the A9 route for commercial purposes. The LTTE levied a tax on such goods at the entry point into Vanni. Traders attempted to evade this tax and were sometimes caught, rightly or wrongly. Taxation-related complaints also petered out once the A9 route was closed by the Lankan Military. In essence, NESoHR's work was dominated by complaints against recruitment by the LTTE. Some examples will clarify the issue.

In 2005 the seventeen-year-old son of a single mother was placed at the education center run by TRO. This was the same education center referred to in the first chapter. The mother of this boy wanted him back home, but the son refused to return. The case was presented to NESoHR by LTTE as giving the boy an education versus sending the boy home to be an assistant to the mother's brother who was an electrician. It was said that this uncle wanted the boy back because he was an assistant whom he was training, and the mother supported him. The boy saw it differently, probably encouraged by those at the education center, and insisted that he needed to study for his GCE-O/L examination. The mother staged a sit-in for few days on her own at the NESoHR office, accepting its hospitality too. When asked why she was against her son's education, she said that she knew what the LTTE meant by educating the boy, but if ever there was another war, she did not want her son to be sent to fight. This conversation took place in early 2005, and the chances of another war seemed remote to me then, but not to this mother. The mother gave up her struggle after a few days because the seventeen-year-old refused to go with her.

Ian Martin, the former Director of Amnesty International, was the human rights advisor to the 2002 ceasefire agreement-based peace process. He had made a few earlier visits to Kilinochchi after the ceasefire, but his visit in 2005 was his last visit before full-scale war erupted. These were the days when the issue of child soldiers within the LTTE dominated the peace process. The LTTE had obviously decided to stage a media coup by releasing a fair number of underage recruits through NESoHR while Ian Martin visited the office. Even the UNICEF Head of Kilinochchi was invited. The NESoHR office was chock-a-block with the underage recruits waiting to be released, their families waiting to take them home, and of course the ever-present Vanni media. I do not think there were outside media for Ian Martin's visit at that time.

The parents and the released recruits were seated. Ian Martin, UNICEF-Kilinochchi head, NESoHR members, and the LTTE person in charge of the release were seated in front of the parents. The aim was to facilitate free conversation between the visitors and the families. I heard some commotion in a side room and went in. One of the girls to be released, a sixteen-year-old, was there with some NESoHR employees. I was then told that this girl did not wish to return with her family. Looking back I am not sure if this was staged, but I, too, was being drawn into the drama, just like the visitors. However, the girl's refusal to go with her family was genuine, I do not doubt it. Someone told her to go and talk to the visitors about her wish, which she did, making Ian Martin feel awkward. I requested that UNICEF take over the case, but after talking to the girl, the UNICEF staff just left without taking any steps. The father of the girl attempted to physically drag her away, but was prevented by many, including myself. It seemed wrong to place a sixteen-year-old girl crying out for help back with her family when there was strong suspicion of abuse. The girl refused to be placed in any other child-care institution and insisted on going to an LTTE base for girls. She was handed to the women's political division for an abode and for completing her GCE-O/L examination, which she did. I was told that she later joined the movement.

A very young, full-term pregnant mother expecting her second child came with a complaint in 2006. She was seeking leave for her husband, who was with LTTE's paid auxiliary force. These were paid soldiers employed by the LTTE, but they were not fully fledged LTTE members. She wanted her husband to be with her for the birth of their child. Her request was not in order to have her husband's moral support during childbirth, rather to have his physical help to travel the long distance from her very remote village in Vanni to the nearest hospital by bullock cart when she started to have labor pains. Apparently the authorities had refused him leave. NESoHR recommended leave for her husband, but I am not sure what the outcome was.

Another case in 2005 involved a young sixteen-year-old Tamil boy from a Diaspora family. The boy was going off the rails in the West. His family had sent him to Vanni to be with the LTTE in order to learn about the real world. He was meant to be attached to the international division of the LTTE and not join the movement as such. But LTTE also had an appetite for young Tamils educated in the West. This particular young boy had promised to someone in the LTTE international division that he would join the movement. However, he later changed his mind when his family visited him in Kilinochchi. The boy was free to go because he was under age, but one of the LTTE members in the international division acted rudely towards the family, and there was a war of words between this LTTE member and the older brother of the boy in question. The family came to NESoHR to lodge a complaint about the conduct of the LTTE member. The older brother of the family threatened to go public. Alarmed at what this might mean because the boy in question was under age, even Pulitheevan, the head of the Peace Secretariat, stepped in and had a diplomatic conversation with the older brother. The family left happily, except for the older brother. He was fuming because he felt insulted by the LTTE member in the international division and had no qualms about taking revenge by holding out his little brother as one example of child soldier recruitment, though this was not really the case.

Another child, Mathan, was forcefully recruited when he was twelve years old, but was released with other very young children in the late 1990s. Mathan was recruited again when he was sixteen in 2003. The family came to NESoHR when Mathan was eighteen years old and a well-trained member of LTTE. They said the family had been barred from meeting him for two years. They sought NESoHR's assistance only to see their son. Mathan visited the family almost a year after the family approached NESoHR. He made a few more visits to the family since, and the family was indeed proud of the way he had turned out. Mathan was killed in action 2006. These are a sample of cases from this period that stand out in my mind.

The UN Convention on the Rights of the Child was declared in 1989, where the age limit for taking part in armed conflict was set at fifteen. Its Optional Protocol on Children Affected by Armed Conflict was declared in 2001, where the age limit remained the same, but an additional clause to this protocol set the age limit for non-state armed actors at eighteen. In Sri Lanka, UNICEF began monitoring the recruitment of those under the age of eighteen by non-state actors, mainly the LTTE.

Following the 2002 ceasefire, UNICEF signed an Action Plan in 2003 with LTTE to release and rehabilitate child soldiers. The local NGO, TRO functioning under LTTE patronage, was its local implementation partner. Several other international NGOs also joined the plan as implementation partners. SLMM and ICRC also independently started monitoring underage recruitment. In 2005, the UN Security Council declared Resolution 1612, also on Children Affected by Armed Conflict. The Resolution 1612 mandated monitoring bodies in selected countries to monitor underage recruitment. UNICEF was mandated to monitor underage recruitment in Sri Lanka, and SLMM was also included in this 1612 monitoring task.

In the heyday of child soldier releases, getting funding for child soldiers was such a lucrative business for international NGOs, that they all wanted a part of it. The Action Plan took off with much media hype, but the implementation was frustrating to the released child soldiers and their families. These young people had become used to the life with LTTE that offered good food, occupation, discipline, and camaraderie. The rehabilitation program put in place by the international NGOs failed to rehabilitate the released children back into the civilian society. The LTTE said most of the released child soldiers were returning back to them, causing them a big headache. The LTTE accused the international NGOs of wasting the huge amounts of funds obtained for this rehabilitation and it unofficially withdrew from the Action Plan. Indeed a study commissioned by UNICEF in 2007 about this Action Plan found implementation problems due to the lack of coordination among the international NGO implementation partners.

The opening of NESoHR provided another venue for the LTTE to publicly release child soldiers, but UNICEF held onto the role it had gained through the Action Plan and kept hammering at LTTE to revitalize it. In this ongoing LTTE child soldier story, I had another role which will be revisited later in the book.

Human rights education was another catch phrase in those early days of the 2002 ceasefire. It seemed everyone needed to be informed of human rights—LTTE personnel, LTTE police personnel, NESoHR staff, school children, and the general public. There were grants to be obtained for it too. It looked as if someone out there was thinking that it would help the peace process. I remember reading in the news at that time, that some Western countries had given large sums of money to the Lankan government to train the Lankan Military on human rights. During my activism in New Zealand, I received a letter from the Australian Foreign

Ministry in 2002 saying that as part of Australia's effort to promote the peace process, they had given a large sum of money to the Lankan government for human rights training of its military.

There was consternation in NESoHR when HUDEC, a Catholic Humanitarian NGO, once announced that it was going to conduct human rights classes for some senior Tamil employees in the Lankan local government departments in Vanni. I am not sure why it caused consternation, but I could see that at NESoHR people felt that it should be conducted by NESoHR. It was obvious to me that NESoHR's capacity was woefully inadequate to do such a job. It turned out that none of the groups interested in this job had the kind of resources required to raise human rights awareness. NESoHR did, however, conduct a few classes lead by Kili-father.

In reality, a true understanding of the human rights ideals requires not only familiarity with the various human rights instruments but also an understanding of its workings in the real world. In other words, how human rights are implemented through national human rights bodies, international human rights bodies, and UN bodies etc. Such an understanding cannot be gained without being able to read English. The availability of Tamil translations of the human rights instruments were and probably still are minimal. UN agencies in Vanni had circulated translations of some of the UN human rights instruments, but they were in an atrocious language style and were almost unreadable. Even standardized terms for Charter, Convention, Covenant and Protocol did not exist to teach the human rights instruments in Tamil. Without the depth in available reading material on human rights, I did not believe human rights awareness could be brought about by such classes.

I was interested in recruiting the assistance of capable GCE-A/L students to record details of some of the major pre-2002 massacres by the Lankan Military. We were hoping to use this to write detailed reports on them. To this end, we went and talked to the students in two schools—a boys school and a girls school. This approach never took off because of inadequate follow up with the students. One experience during these class meetings is worth noting because this tendency could be noted readily in several other circumstances. In order to give the girls an understanding of the purpose of the project, we showed them one report NESoHR had already produced and read small parts of it. In that report we had used the term *Thalaiyaaddi*. The word literally means the one who nods his head in the typically South Asian style to convey agreement. This word had taken on a special meaning in contemporary Tamil, and was used with this special meaning in casual conversations. *Thalaiyaaddi* meant a hooded Tamil informer used by the Lankan Military to pick out the LTTE members and supporters from a line-up by nodding their head—and thus the popular usage of the term. The purpose of the hooded mask was to protect the informer from LTTE assassination. The intelligent girls in this "good" school did not know the meaning conveyed by this term. That this ignorance was gender related dawned on me later after similar experiences. At that time I was quite angry that these intelligent girls were ignorant of such matters. In reality, boys had a greater awareness of events in the political arena than the girls, who had a much more secluded upbringing.

The US embassy contacted NESoHR twice. Once it requested statistical data on the complaints that were being handled by NESoHR. The embassy also invited Kili-father once for a meeting in Colombo. The preparation of statistical data for the US embassy caused a lot a commotion within NESoHR. Kili-father took personal interest in the final data sheet that was prepared. It seems there was much sensitivity related to presenting statistics on the complaints of underage recruitment. I did not see why this should be an issue, because I thought underage recruits were being released when complaints were received. Later on I had reason to doubt that LTTE was fully co-operating with NESoHR on this matter at that time.

Once, a very old man from Trincomalee visited NESoHR. He had come all the way from Trincomalee, and he had in his possession a lot of documents relating to his land and some letters from the Sansoni Commission of the 1970s offering him compensation for his losses during the pogroms against the Tamils. It is a historical fact that he, and indeed all others like him, never received the compensation recommended by the commission. That was the first time I heard in person from someone so old about his long years of waiting for his grievances to be addressed. It gave a new dimension to my understanding of the plight of Tamils. Such pogroms against the Tamils with the support of the Lankan armed forces had been occurring with regular frequency from 1956 until 1983. Following the 1983 pogrom Tamil armed movements grew in strength and the pogroms ceased to occur. Since then the violence against Tamils was perpetrated in the name of fighting the armed groups.

We also received the family of a *kiraama-seevakar*, a Lankan local government employee, from Jaffna, who was allegedly arrested by the LTTE and remained missing. Such cases against the LTTE invariably fell into the hands of Kili-father, and it was difficult for me to extract the truth about it. I can only guess that this *kiraama-seevakar* was arrested because he was working with the Lankan Military in Jaffna. I do not know if he was eventually released or disappeared.

Several attempts during the early days of NESoHR to set up branch offices in other districts never materialized. Suspicion that recorded complaints against the LTTE might fall into the wrong hands and be used to further demonize LTTE was a prevailing fear.

By December 2005 two of NESoHR's founding members,

Chanthira Nehru from Amparai and Joseph Pararajasingam from Batticaloa, had been killed by the Lankan-affiliated forces. Their pictures hung in the visitors' hall of NESoHR in Kilinochchi. Chanthira Nehru was killed in February 2005 as he returned from Vanni to Amparai after meeting Thamilselvan to discuss work related to the 2004 December tsunami. He was in the car with Batticaloa LTTE Political Head Kousalyan, and they were both killed. Joseph Pararajasingam was killed in December 2005 while he attended the Christmas mass conducted by the Bishop of Batticaloa, Kingsley Swampillai, in a church in Batticaloa town. His body was brought to Vanni. I was with Kili-father at the Vanni border to receive the body early one afternoon. We returned to Kilinochchi in procession with the body. The long procession stopped at several places, and took eight hours to reach Kilinochchi center. As we drove through the night through uninhabited parts of road, lone figures of women stood in the dark with flowers to pay respect. The procession never failed to stop for them. Those gestures said more about Pararajasingam, the person of the people, than the organized meetings. Later in April 2008, when Kili-father was killed, the outpouring of grief by the most downtrodden was even louder. Once we displaced from Kilinochchi in 2008 and set up office in Puthukkudiyiruppu, pictures of all three hung in the one room office.

December 2005 saw a major shift in NESoHR's focus due to the sharp rise in disappearances and murders in the Lankan-controlled areas of Tamil Eelam, especially in Jaffna. The families of victims, in desperation, went around lodging the incidents with every possible authority that was prepared to record it. The Lankan Human Rights Commission, Lankan Police, International Committee of the Red Cross (ICRC), Sri Lanka Monitoring Mission (SLMM) and a few other human rights organizations, including NESoHR, were the common port of call for these families. While the A9 route remained opened, these families had easy access to NESoHR, and we issued reports on each incident that was directly reported to us.

The first of such reports was the rape and murder of a girl from an islet off the Jaffna peninsula. This was quickly followed by many more reports on abductions, killings, and disappearances. We could not keep pace with the incidents. We met in person with family members of victims from Jaffna who had been abducted by paramilitary groups with overt help from the Lankan Military. The collaboration between the paramilitary group and the Lankan Military was so obvious, and the victims' families saw it clearly. However, despite the huge presence of international agencies in Jaffna, most of whom directly received these complaints from families, this collaboration was never widely reported. A few months into 2006, Vanni was isolated with the closure of the A9 route. Disappearances and extrajudicial killings in Tamil Eelam under Lankan control rose to a climax over the next two years, but remained unreported.

6

Documentation

As a member of the Tamil Diaspora in New Zealand, I had been an activist for a few years prior to my time in Vanni. During this period, I had felt there was an acute lack of adequate in-depth information on what was happening in the Tamil homeland. Once I started working at NESoHR and was exposed to people with personal experiences of oppression and war, I realized that a lot of their experiences had not been told to the rest of the world, including the Tamil Diaspora. I had a strong urge to write about it, and there was so much one could write about. My documentation efforts that began with NESoHR continued throughout my four-year stay in Vanni, quite independent of my other projects.

An old couple, whose three young sons disappeared in a single incident in August 1990, visited NESoHR in 2005. The parents insisted that their three sons were still alive somewhere, and sought NESoHR's help to find them. Their perseverance was deeply moving and I was handed the first heart-wrenching war experience that I had to write about. We launched the project to investigate the disappearances which took place on the islets off the Jaffna peninsula in three adjacent villages. The incident took place over a period of one month during a Lankan Military operation against the LTTE. Early on in our investigations, we were handed a list of names of seventy young men who had disappeared during that period. The list had been prepared by a Tamil senior local government official for that area immediately after the disappearances. During the military operation, the Lankan Military had taken away hundreds of young men from their families, as they sought refuge in churches and temples, to be used for forced labor. Most of these young men later returned to their families but more than seventy never returned. Informed sources from these villages believed that these men were tortured and killed to avenge the losses faced by the Lankan Military in the operation. As our investigations progressed, we added more names to the original list.

For me it was an extraordinary experience in many ways. Kili-father was my partner in the project. He organized the affected people to come and meet me in his parish church in Naavanthurai in Jaffna. We had two such meetings with the people, and to me just staying at the church residence among the Catholic people was a rewarding experience. Listening to the stories people recited was part of an ongoing process of enlightenment for me that started with the visits to children's home with Karan in 2004 and continued throughout my stay in Vanni. Every time families recited their traumatic experiences, they lived through it again. Many of them cried out loud recollecting events of more than a decade ago. They always did so in the hope that the one listening to them, especially if it was a well-known group, would help them find answers. Was it fair to make them live through it again? Were we really helping them? Though documenting such history is important for the community as a whole, on an individual basis the benefits to the families are hard to see. I felt that I was put through an exceptional experience for which I owed them much. I poured my soul into writing the NESoHR report which we called the MA-M³ report abbreviating Mandaithiivu-Allaipiddi-Mankumbaan, the three villages adjacent to each other where these disappearances took place over a period one month.

I have since heard directly from many mothers, fathers, wives and siblings about the murder and disappearance of their family members. In the vast majority of cases, these family members were males in their prime, who would have brought income and support to their families. Most of the families were very poor and the economic loss of an earning member was felt deeply. In several cases the disappeared family member would have been the only breadwinner in the family, thus pushing the family to destitution; something I observed while talking to the children in the children's homes and the beneficiaries in the many welfare institutions for women. I also observed that the suffering of the families of the disappeared was unparalleled. Due to the uncertainty of their fate, the family's grieving never ends. I have felt this pain of the families acutely. I would have just loved to spend the rest of my life documenting such traumas of the voiceless people because I had no other power than just that. At that time, I was convinced that my call for then in Vanni was the documentation of the immediate past history of the people.

Sometime in 2004 an organization, the Statistical Centre for North East (SNE), was formed in Vanni. With the help of Jaffna University staff, it had embarked on a project to collect war-related statistics—on the occupation of Tamil land by the Lankan Military and on the Tamil civilian war casualties. The project was nearly completed but was interrupted by the 2004 tsunami. The data had already been drafted into two excellent documents in Tamil. One was on the land occupation, or in other words the High Security Zones, and the other was on the large scale massacres of Tamils.

As soon as I saw these two documents, I realized that they had to be brought out in English through NESoHR. Both of these efforts required a large investment of time, which no one at NESoHR had. The High Security Zone document was the smaller project and NESoHR produced a report in early 2005, focusing only on Jaffna.[4] The High Security Zone data for all the eight districts in the Tamil homeland was later presented at the 2006 Geneva talks by the LTTE Peace Secretariat. As a result, this received some publicity. The term High Security Zone is used by many other states in the world to declare specific areas which are highly security sensitive. These High Security Zone areas are always very small in populated areas, and larger High Security Zone areas are always in remote areas, far away from population centers. In contrast, in the Lankan context this same term was used to describe vast areas in the middle of densely-populated centers in the Tamil homeland. In most cases, people on private property were evicted in order to declare the area as a High Security Zone. These areas were used for no other purpose than to house the vast Sinhala military to oppress the Tamil population. A more accurate term for these areas is Militarized Zones. The Lankan government was continuing to add more and more such areas in the Tamil homeland.

The second report in Tamil produced by the Statistical Centre for North East was the first draft of a report that documented more than one hundred large-scale massacres of Tamils prior to 2002. This too was not published and was in very limited circulation. I began translation work of this report into English and continued even after I left NESoHR in mid-2006. It was released by NESoHR in 2007.[5] I wrote another smaller report for NESoHR in mid-2008, describing the massacres that had taken place after 2002.[6] The Tamil report remained unpublished and it went through many more revisions. It was eventually published on the NESoHR website only in January 2009, under the noise of artillery explosions and flying aerial bombers. It was the last large-scale report released by NESoHR, and it was the result of incessant efforts by Ramanan, who became a very active fulltime co-ordinator of NESoHR following the assassination of Kili-father. By December 2009, Ramanan and I had managed to get out of the island. We started work on combining, polishing, and updating these two reports. Another NESoHR founding member, who had escaped from the island in 2006 following death threats against him, also joined us. Many other Diaspora members also contributed. This combined report was eventually published in December 2009 in India, both in Tamil and English under the title, *Massacres of Tamils, 1956—2008*, by an organization called Manitham. On request from Manitham, the massacres of Tamils committed by the Indian forces stationed in the Tamil homeland during 1987-1989 following the 1987 Indo-Lanka accord were removed from this book. These massacres, by Indian forces, were later published separately in April 2011, also in India by the Delhi Tamil Students Union, as a small booklet.

Another category of statistics collected by the Statistical Centre for North East was on civilians affected by war up to 2002. These were perhaps the best statistics of their type on Tamil civilian casualties that were ever collected, but tragically they have been lost. In 2005, NESoHR published a summary of these statistics as a report.[7] It was the first of its kind and was initially welcomed, but quickly it became the target of protest from members of the Tamil Diaspora because the statistics under-represented the enormity of civilian casualties. The protest persisted despite the fact the report acknowledged that the statistics were incomplete and what was being published had been collected in person through a massive homeland-wide project. Due to this opposition, further publicity based on this data was avoided. I had access to this data in full only in December 2008, and I planned to upload it into the NESoHR website, but failed because the conditions were already deteriorating too fast to do any work of this nature.

The project on civilian statistics also collected more than 2000 affidavits from families about what had happened to their family member(s). There were doubts as to the adequacy of the affidavits as legal documents. Yet NESoHR made some effort to add the English translation, and formalize and digitize these affidavits, but it failed to muster adequate resources to complete the project. This too is now lost.

Following the publication of the detailed report on the disappearances on the islets off Jaffna peninsula, which we called the M-A-M report,[3] we were already planning another detailed report on a massacre. Before this report could be completed, December 2005— the period marking the commencement of an increased seemingly systemic pattern of murders and disappearances—came upon us. This meant the present situation was becoming worse and NESoHR could not afford to waste resources recording the past. NESoHR's clients during this period have already been described in the previous chapter. Within a period of seven months, our access to this category of clients was severely diminished by the closure of the A9 route. Thus, we at NESoHR went back to recording past history as much as we could. We started three projects. One was on a massacre at a village in Piramanthanaaru in Mullaithiivu. This was completed and published.[8] We started another one on a massacre in another village, Pannankandi in Kilinochchi, which was never completed though a lot of data had been collected. A massacre in Othiyamalai was another one that was started. A Diaspora activist produced a report on the massacre by the Indian Peace Keeping Forces in Jaffna in the village of Valvai. This report in turn was based on the first-hand report by a victim. The LTTE prevented NESoHR from publishing this report because nothing against India was to be published at that time. This report is now lost.

In the NESoHR report on the massacre in Piramanthanaaru noted above, we noted a statement by a relative of a victim. In her statement she referred to the presence of a white-skinned mercenary whom she called *"mosaaddu"*, a Tamilized version of Israel's intelligence, Mossad. This relative described how a Lankan Military helicopter landed near her home. The Lankan Military had got out of the helicopter and shot her brother, who was staying with her. They then dragged him into the helicopter never to be seen alive again. She said,

> *"One of them was a tall white man who was watching everything carefully. Many other people in my village saw him that day. Villagers later referred to him as mosaaddu* [Mossad]. *I didn't know what it meant then. Later I learnt that mosaaddu are overseas white men."*

Around the time we were working on the above report, I also heard about a book, *The Reluctant Mercenary*,[9] written by Tim Smith. With some effort I managed to get a copy of this book. Tim Smith was a fighter helicopter pilot. In the book he tells about his role as a mercenary working for the Lankan government in the Tamil homeland. He was hired by an outfit in the United Kingdom in the mid-1980s to train fighter helicopter pilots for the Lankan air force. But once he arrived in Lanka, to his dismay he found himself flying fighter helicopters from which Sinhala Air Force men fired on and killed Tamil women, children, and old people. Tim Smith mentioned several white men, whom he referred to as "white faces" in his book, living at the Palaly Air Force base in Jaffna doing work similar to what he was doing. He referred to the UK outfit that hired him as a buffer to protect the UK intelligence service. What Tim Smith described in his book and what the woman from Piramanthanaaru told us about *"mosaaddu"* fitted together perfectly. For Tim Smith, white men were "white faces", and for the woman they were *"mosaaddu"*.

Tim Smith had written the book years earlier. But the book was published only in 2002, immediately after the 2002 ceasefire. Due to the high hopes following the ceasefire and the frequent rounds of peace talks that followed soon after, this book never gained the popularity it deserved. One cannot hope for better proof of how the UK government of that time helped the Lankan government by sending mercenaries to train them to kill Tamil civilians.

Some of the reports that I helped to prepare touched my soul because I had the opportunity to study the background to the reports in depth. The MAM report, noted earlier, on the disappearances on the islets off the Jaffna coast was the first of its kind. Others include: a report on the war's impact on the fishing community in the Tamil homeland; a report on the demographic changes in the Tamil homeland; the translation of a war diary by an LTTE member, Malaravan; and a report on the eviction of the people from the villages of Kokkilaay, Kokkuththoduvaay, and Karunaaddukkeeni. The last was the one we were working on until January 2009, but it was never completed and published. It too is now lost.

During this period, local news reports on attacks on the fishing community were common. Even when one was just chatting with the Vanni people, the topic of past attacks and disappearances at sea and the loss of a way of life kept coming up. Did the fishing community support the LTTE more than the rest of the Tamils? Or did the Lankan Military's fear of the LTTE Naval Division cause the fishing community to be targeted? Or was the fishing community targeted in order to evict them from the rich fishing coastal areas? I am still not sure. All three could have been reasons for the attacks faced by the Tamil fishing community. But it was clear that this community suffered a lot. There are many songs on the hardships faced by the Tamil fishing community. Some of them are beautifully mournful; an old popular one goes:

When the silvery moon lights the dark sky
And the sea breeze is thick with salty dampness
The little boat with the pile of net goes to sea.
Long time will pass before it returns.

No one knows our pain, no one understands us.
No one hears our mournful songs.

When the village is asleep and no one is around
In the dead of night, we put our boats to sea.
If the Navy sees us, we die in the sea.
Without a name, without the loved ones to know
Our wet body may wash ashore next morning.
Tomorrow the Tigers will change our plight.

Despite the common knowledge of the problems faced by this community, reports on its plight were non-existent. I discussed it with Karan, and in his typical style the long process of the production of a report on the fishing community began instantly.[10] The task was given to a father-son team of visiting Diaspora activists. That was the seed. But their stay was too short for them to continue to flesh it out. In due course I took over. Community leaders from fisher communities around the Tamil homeland came over specifically to talk to us about their issues. I felt privileged and humbled. It was very sad to listen to the older ones reminiscing about a way of life that was lost. Two matters were brought up repeatedly. Tamils were the skilled deep sea fishermen of the island but this had gradually changed and during my stay in Vanni, Tamils did not have permission to own or operate deep sea fishing vessels. Older fishermen reminisced about the exhilaration of going deep sea fishing.

In Jaffna, in particular, women of this community played an equal economic role. Their roles included, among others, selling the catch and processing what was not sold. Another role was the ritual of receiving their husbands returning from a day or more at sea. A woman would stand on the beach with a "bottle of tea" (it needed to be a bottle with a lid to keep it hot and clean). She would then prepare a meal on the beach itself, under a rudimentary hut without walls, the *vaadi*. This meal was called *puliyaanam* and was made with rice and the best fish from the catch the husband had just brought, spiced with many other things. The Lankan Military had banned all of these practices. It would be very rewarding to write an updated report on these same communities. I very much miss the opportunity to do so.

As the fuel shortage began to bite in 2007 due to the Lankan embargo on fuel, I was left with long hours without electricity. I began to visit an LTTE library near the Peace Secretariat and the LTTE bookshop, *Arivamathu*, in Kilinochchi. I made an attempt to study as much of the available LTTE literature as possible that would hold my attention. I became a fan of one young writer, Malaravan, who had been killed in battle in 1990. Before he reached the age of twenty, Malaravan had already written two excellent short novels and two books of poetry. I liked Malaravan because his writing was directed at the most ordinary members as well as the civilians. During his brief membership with the LTTE, he had been in charge of the Jaffna student section of the LTTE. During this time he wrote the short novel *Puyal Paravai*. In this novel he takes on the subject of women's liberation and female membership in the LTTE. It is an astounding work for a 20-year-old Jaffna male of that time. His other short novel is *War Journey (Poor ulaa)*. I translated this short novel using paper and pencil during those hours when there was no electricity. I typed it when there were short hours of electricity. A female LTTE friend designed a book cover and made a map with the place names appearing in the book. There this effort seemed to have remained since 2007. To my pleasant surprise, I was contacted by a friend in India in 2010 to be told that Penguin India had agreed to publish the translation.

The demographic change to the Tamil homeland is an issue that has received some attention recently, following the 2007 takeover by the government of the land belonging to the Tamils in Sampoor, Trincomalee. The process of demographic change in Tamil Eelam has a six-decade-long history, and yet it has not been well documented except for some very brief notes in Tamil. Solid data on this was not available. I heard of one person, Vipulenthiran, who had made it his life goal to document this. Vipulenthiran left his education in the medical college to join the LTTE. Recording the history of land occupation in the Tamil homeland was his lifelong project. He was the son of a senior local government employee from Trincomalee, an area where Tamils have suffered much due to these planned demographic changes. He thus had means of access to data. I heard of his work and was eager to do a report in English because he was working on a Tamil book. Understandably he did not want to divulge anything until his book was released, and it did take a further two years before the book came out in early 2008.

As soon as his book, *Thamileela ellaiyai nookki nagaruvoom* (*Let us move towards the borders of Tamil Eelam*), came out I set to work on an English report, basing it on his book as well as the other brief notes that existed in Tamil. Using statistical data on demography collected since 1881 the report showed the steady incursion of Sinhala settlements in the areas that were recognized even by earlier colonial governments as Tamil areas. One of the most striking changes in demography was recorded in the Trincomalee district. In 1881, Tamils represented 80% of the population of this district. This continues to decrease to this day and currently is less than 35%. I value this report[11] because it filled a gap in available documented data on this topic.

In late 2008, while still in Kilinochchi, Ramanan and I decided that the best way to use our resources at that stage would be to work on a large-scale report. We decided on documenting the 1980s eviction of Tamils from Kokkilaay-Kokkuththoduvaay-Karunaaddukkeeni villages because no in-depth reporting of this existed. These villages join the Trincomalee and Mullaithiivu districts. Ilankumaran (Baby Subramanium), well known for his habit of collecting and keeping old documents, had some very valuable books on this. The uprooted people of these villages lived in the Mullaithiivu district, and they had their memories as well as some documents. We set about our work, and the people of this village gave us full support. One of the books Ilankumaran gave us was written in the 1830s by a British colonial administrator about the area, and it was rich in fascinating information. One LTTE member originally from this area produced some Google Map pictures showing the contrast between their villages which were now covered with overgrown bushes and the new adjacent Sinhala settlements with wide new roads. We also collected some photographs of the villagers in front of their dilapidated buildings. These photographs were taken by them when the Lankan Military took them back to their villages in the early 1990s during one brief period of ceasefire. Ilankumaran also gave us the voters list for this electorate before and after the Sinhala settlements, which clearly showed the deliberate manipulation of the electorate. We were quite excited by the progress. But since this report was still in progress in early 2009, we lost it in the ensuing chaos.

7

Vanni media

I want to interrupt the description of my experiences in NESoHR and the Peace Secretariat with a description of the Vanni media. This is of relevance to the following chapters. I have already described the pervasive rituals of Vanni under the LTTE. The LTTE media functioning in Vanni was another substantive dimension of the Vanni social space. LTTE media also had a pervasive presence in Vanni. *Eelanaatham* daily newspaper and *Pulikalin-kural* (Voice of Tigers) radio service both had a long history under the LTTE. Through their pervasive presence, these two media bonded with people who had no other means of long distance communication—there was no private telephone or internet access. Conversations in public places often referred to stories appearing in these two media.

Eelanaatham was supposed to be a civilian newspaper and not an official organ of the LTTE. As far as the ordinary people were concerned it was a paper that never criticized any of the actions of the LTTE. It was also the most popular newspaper. *Eelanaatham* was a morning paper. The headlines were always either political or military news. No other news could ever make it to the headlines. Though papers from Jaffna and Colombo reached Vanni at this time, *Eelanaatham* was still the most widely read newspaper because it had the greatest volume of local news and local writing. It also was the cheapest. People routinely stopped in front of the distribution outlets in the mornings to buy the paper—there was no home delivery. People would scan the front page anxiously, either to find the latest political news or the latest military news, before putting it in their bicycle basket and riding away.

Until the war loomed large from 2006 onward, the headlines were mostly about news on the peace process, mostly on the meetings held between LTTE and the peace-makers. The remainder of the paper carried a lot of local news about the inadequacy of services in the public space. This ranged from the poor conditions of the roads and lanes, to stray animal problems in public spaces such as temples, to the urgent need for classroom spaces for schools. When one read the paper, one felt like it was the mouthpiece of the people, talking to the authorities—both to the LTTE and to the local Lankan government departments. Except for these highly localized issues, the paper focused almost exclusively on the politico-military aspects of the struggle. I cannot remember larger social issues, such as the women's issue, being covered in the paper during this time. The paper clearly reflected the mood of a people coming out of a war and being hopeful and absorbed in the peace process.

The shift to a war-centered coverage in *Eelanaatham* started sometime in 2006. There were special evening deliveries to mark special events. It happened twice during my stay there. Once, when for the very first time, an LTTE plane flew into Colombo, dropped bombs and flew back. The other was when there was a very successful Black Tiger attack on the Anuraathapuram Air Force airport, destroying more than twenty fighter planes and helicopters. The crowds at the paper distribution centers for these special evening editions were amazing. The paper would be sold out in no time.

The tabloid-sized *Eelanaatham,* which was published daily, also issued a special edition on Fridays named *Vellinaatham*, emphasizing the "Friday" in its name. This carried at least five or six full-page articles. The number of writers who contributed was limited and the same writers wrote again and again. From about 2008, there were a series of articles with a generic title "a voice from inside" that spoke of the emotions, thoughts, and experiences of the fighters on the battlelines. There were both female and male writers reporting from female and male units. These were very popular.

Eelanaatham was dominated by males. Female journalists in *Eelanaatham* were rare. There was one very brave female journalist, a short plump woman, who even reported from very near the front lines. She took some of the best photographs for the paper. Compared to *Eelanaatham, Pulikalin-kural* had a much larger group of female contributors, and it was probably due to the people running the institution rather than any other reason. Perhaps females also did a better job as radio announcers than as reporters.

Pulikalin-kural had a broader reach than *Eelanaatham* because it carried music. LTTE music filled this radio service. *Pulikalin-kural* had a unique way to encourage listening. There was a year-long program of questions on the history of the Tamil struggle for which *Pulikalin-kural* would receive answers from listeners. Regularly it would announce winners. Younger female members were the most ardent participants in this program.

The very first early morning *Pulikalin-kural* news was followed by a five-minute program called *Maattam* (Change). When the program was launched it took up highly ideological themes aimed at changing social norms that were out of sync with modern world, which was refreshing. Women's issues dominated the topics covered. However, later, as the war became intense, out of necessity the program became all about the war and the need to support the war.

There were many other attractions in *Pulikalin-kural*. A serialized radio drama cum soap, *Paathai* (Path), was religiously followed by civilians and LTTE members, young and old alike. The *Pulikalin-kural* radio service reached even the Diaspora through the internet, which the *Eelanatham* newspaper did not do. It would be negligent not to mention Iraivan, a regular *Pulikalin-kural* contributor, who took on many roles within *Pulikalin-kural*. Iraivan was an institution in his own right, and he did reach the people. Many older men were ardent followers of Iraivan and would not miss his programs. He was the anchor of the daily morning program *Naalithalnaali*, an analysis of morning newspapers from around the island. He also presented a detailed analysis of current events every day. Iraivan's fate after May 2009 remains unknown.

A national television, NTT (National Television of Tamil Eelam), was started sometime in 2005. Filming had always been one of the active divisions within the LTTE. Some members were specifically trained to be cameramen and video editors, and they had become very good at this. The LTTE was also renowned for filming at the front lines during battles. Indeed, there were quite a few *maaveerar* who were killed while filming battles. *Oliveechchu* was a collection of video programs that were put together approximately on a monthly basis for Diaspora viewing. After the 2002 ceasefire, the *Oliveechchu* series was abandoned in favor of television because the technology was now more readily available to reach the Diaspora through television. Even before the launch of the television channel NTT, another team within the international division of the LTTE had started to produce television programs that were sent to the Diaspora outlets to be broadcast on the Tamil Diaspora channels. NTT, however, was also a local television watched by the people in Vanni. I was amazed at the number of different teams that were producing television programs without much co-ordination among themselves, and the amount of resources being used as a result. It seemed that no one could resist the chance to do filming and produce programs.

Oliveechchu was not the only casualty of NTT. The road shows, *therukkooththu*, also came to an end with NTT, as television sets were installed in public places and people gathered at night to watch. Vanni had indeed entered the modern era. NTT was broadcast for only four hours at night, but the programs were varied and entertaining. However, the intervals between programs were long and these were filled with LTTE music videos, which were always militaristic and war oriented. Some of the programs on NTT attracted mass audiences, and among these were political satires admirably acted by a sixty-or-so-year-old, very unusual female LTTE member. Sometime in 2006, Thamilselvan pushed for and started an English program division within NTT, which ended up doing only a fifteen minute news service. One popular, multi-talented NTT personality was Isaipiriya. She was brutally raped and murdered by the Lankan forces at the end of the war in May 2009, and video evidence of this is now publicly available.

Eelanaatham, Pulikalin-kural, and NTT together irresistibly drew the Vanni population, both the civilian and the member-community, into the LTTE mode of thinking. The resources poured into them probably did not justify the purpose, if it was to draw the population into the LTTE fold insofar as the population by default was already with the LTTE at this time. The NTT was achieving a different goal, which was to inject national pride by the mere fact of having a national television. It was seen as a step towards the fulfilment of the Tamil nation becoming a state. It also substituted for *Oliveechchu* and the road shows admirably. Overall, *Pulikalin-kural* focused more on the social sphere, and *Eelanaatham* on the political sphere. On the other hand the NTT appeared to focus on the military sphere by an overwhelming portrayal of members in military fatigue promoting militarism. This may have been due to its time of birth when war was already imminent.

As this period progressed, all three media came under pressure from Lankan authorities in many forms. *Eelanaatham* suffered from a shortage of printing ink. The NTT suffered when its satellite provider in the United States withdrew the facility, stopping its direct broadcast to Diaspora Tamils all over the world. The service showed remarkable staying power by broadcasting by alternate means. The transmission tower of *Pulikalin-kural* was bombed and destroyed twice, once in 2006 and again in 2007. The headquarters of *Pulikalin-kural* was also bombed on Maaveerar Day in 2007, causing extensive damage and killing many employees. Despite these attacks, as far as I know *Pulikalin-kural* never stopped broadcasting until the end. However, both *Eelanaatham* and NTT were forced to stop functioning once Kilinochchi was evacuated in late 2008.

There were at least four other print media. *Viduthalai Pulikal,* considered the official organ of the LTTE, and *Suthanthira Paravaikal,* considered the official organ of the women's wing of the LTTE. In addition, *Velichcham,* a weekly magazine, contained articles on the experiences of the common people. Old editions of *Velichcham* in particular had a large volume of first-hand descriptions of human rights violations by Lankan authorities faced by the people over the decades. I was once handed a bound volume of some old editions from which I learned a great deal about past atrocities. It also had some good art. A much smaller publication, *Alai,* targeted LTTE members only.

During this period, Vanni was struggling to supply the insatiable demand for quality journalists and writers that the growing number of media outlets demanded. Apprenticeship was encouraged and a media school was started, but the shortage was acute. Yet the performance of the media units was commendable given the resources. The few regular writers were under pressure to produce more, and by working hard, they did. Though I too was frequently asked to contribute, I made only a minor contribution, but I benefited from this exercise because my Tamil writing and typing skills improved immensely.

It was interesting to observe that anti-castism was never discussed in the media. It seems this had already been dealt with and progress had been made. Harping on it was considered a step backwards rather than progressive; especially when some of the senior LTTE leaders, as well as the juniors, were from all types of castes. Love marriages, as opposed to arranged marriages, were more common within the LTTE compared to the rest of the Tamil community. Castism, though not entirely eradicated, seemed to be on the way out in Vanni.

One incident I experienced drove this point home to me very clearly. I did not have my own transport in Vanni except for a brief period after I learned how to ride a scooter. I quickly gave up the scooter because I found it difficult to deal with the roads and traffic in Vanni. Thus most of my transport was provided by the LTTE Peace Secretariat vehicle. I thus came to know the drivers well. They were all civilians of well above average intelligence, and came from families that were strong supporters of the LTTE. I found talking to them to be very educative, and we would chat a lot during our rides about many things concerning Vanni. It never dawned on me to wonder what castes they came from, and we always chatted as social equals. During early 2005, when the A9 route remained opened, I made several trips to Jaffna and I stayed with a family friend. The incident occurred when the LTTE Peace Secretariat vehicle was to pick me up from Jaffna to return to Vanni. The driver and the vehicle arrived at my friend's house, and there was a short delay before I was ready to get into the car. I asked the driver to come into the house and wait while I got ready. He refused and his mannerism was starkly different to his usual mannerism. He conveyed to me through his body language that the people in that home would not want to welcome him into their house if they knew about his caste. It was the typical refusal of a person aware of his lowly caste and the inappropriateness of his associating as an equal with members of the higher caste. It then dawned on me that he was forced to be caste conscious in Jaffna, but did not have to be in the circles he moved in, in Vanni.

It was thus not surprising that this subject was never raised either in the media or in private in Vanni. The lack of caste consciousness within the LTTE was genuine and refreshing, and it would have been one of the leading light achievements of the LTTE, if LTTE society had not been destroyed. This would have been so even if the LTTE failed to achieve an independent Tamil Eelam.

The Lankan government strictly controlled and impeded the entry of reporters from outside media into Vanni. Such reporters only made occasional visits. The LTTE, too, would not have permitted the presence of anyone who wrote consistently negative reports about their governance. Thus, the majority of reports about Vanni reached the outside world through Tamil Diaspora-based internet news websites and the occasional press releases and reports issued by the UN and other international agencies that were freely functioning. The Tamil news websites were always referred to in international circles as pro-LTTE websites, thus diminishing the impact of the news reported in them. The outcome of the partial media blackout throughout this period was that the world more or less remained in the dark concerning the Tamil situation and their perspective on it, even during the time when a ceasefire was in effect.

8

Educating the peacemakers

When I began my long stay in Vanni in March 2005, it was two months after the 2004 Boxing Day tsunami. By then the peace process had stalled, and those in power in Colombo were hardliners—the Lankan prime minister who signed the 2002 ceasefire agreement with LTTE had lost the parliamentary elections in 2004. The efforts of the international community, particularly Norway, to fire up the peace process continued. Many new INGOs sprouted in Vanni, eager to have their hand in the post-tsunami rebuilding. The fascination of the academics with Vanni and the LTTE continued. As a result of all of this, there was no end to the stream of visitors. Though the majority of these visitors were from the West, there was a smattering of people from the rest of the world too. No official Lankan government delegation ever visited Vanni; all direct talks were held in cities outside the island; there were, however, some Sinhalese delegations.

The idea that LTTE promoted human rights fascinated all of these visitors, and they all made it a point to pay a visit to NESoHR. Thus, a lot of our time at NESoHR was spent preparing for and holding meetings with these VIP and non-VIP visitors. Though my initial full-time role at NESoHR was only for about one year, due to the continuous stream of visitors I did meet a number of VIPs who came through Kilinochchi. Sometimes these meetings were together with Kili-father, but there were quite a few without Kili-father because during this time he also had a full-time parish responsibility in Naavanthurai in Jaffna, and thus could not be available for some of the NESoHR meetings in Kilinochchi. I am not sure what these meetings at NESoHR really achieved. No doubt the academics learned something to put in their academic papers and journalists also could put a sentence or two in their news reports based on what they heard at NESoHR. The meetings with three other categories of visitors—UN delegations; Amnesty International (AI) and Human Rights Watch delegations; and Norwegian representatives—exhibited a sharp power distance and the outcomes of these meetings were less obvious.

The very first meeting with a Western representative after the official opening of NESoHR was with the Norwegian ambassador of that time. Kili-father asked me to be present with him at this meeting and candidly explained to me why he needed another person with him at the meeting. He said that he needed another person to take over the conversation so that he could have brief moments to catch his breath and manage his perspiration resulting from nervousness. There were only three of us at the meeting including the ambassador. The discussion, as always, was on the child soldiers. It had an atmosphere that I found common to all official meetings with Western representatives that were taking place in Vanni which I had the opportunity to observe.

As I watched the conversation between Kili-father and the ambassador, I felt sad and angry. Kili-father was a Catholic priest who had dedicated his life to the most downtrodden in Tamil Eelam and for that matter on the entire island. I had seen Lankan Military commanders embracing him at checkpoints. The ambassador, whatever his human qualities were, was there as the highly paid employee of a Western state, echoing the views of the West. What was it that made Kili-father nervous and sweaty about talking to the ambassador? In due course, I came see the power distance that was at work—the power distance between the people of Tamil Eelam and the West. Lofty human qualities meant little in these interactions; these meetings were indeed power dances. In due course I was able to also notice such power dances in other official meetings between the West and Vanni institutions. The representatives of the West were always able to exert power by selectively using some document—an international instrument—to subdue the Vanni representatives.

A Human Rights Watch expert on children, Jo Becker, visited Vanni in 2005. The organization had just published a book, *Living in fear: child soldiers and the Tamil Tigers in Sri Lanka*, which she authored. The web postings on the Human Rights Watch website about Sri Lanka at that time also were almost entirely about the LTTE child soldier issue. At NESoHR, we asked her whether Human Rights Watch considered these to be the gravest human rights violations on the island at that time. She responded by saying that they had just chosen this issue to be their focus. We pointed out to her that a large number of Western organizations had also taken this as their focus at that time. We challenged her to come out on the street to carry out a spot survey asking the people about their perceptions of what were the gravest human rights violations they were facing. She threatened to walk out of the meeting and Kili-father had to pacify her.

An Amnesty International delegation, headed by its director of that time, Irene Khan, visited Vanni and NESoHR. One might have wondered why it was considered necessary for Amnesty International's top executive to visit Vanni. The meeting at NESoHR again was heated because the visiting delegation was so focused on the child soldier issue, at the expense of all other human rights violations that the people were facing. Amnesty International's South Asian representative, Purna Sen, who was in the delegation, switched the topic to the problems facing women and suddenly I found myself crossing over to her side as some male members in the NESoHR team tried to defend the Tamil culture's position on women.

The UN Special Rapporteur on Extrajudicial Killing, Philip Alston, visited NESoHR as part of his official visit to Sri Lanka in November 2005. Extrajudicial executions of LTTE members and supporters in Batticaloa by the Karunaa faction that had split from the LTTE were already pandemic. We at NESoHR read his report[12] closely following this visit. We were perturbed that he failed to identify the Karunaa phenomenon for what it was, even though his visit took place eighteen months after the Karunaa split from the LTTE, and by then the real nature of the Karunaa group was crystal clear to all Tamils. In that report, Alston also rejected the label "paramilitary" given to another armed group in Jaffna, which was known by the acronym EPDP. For us at NESoHR, who had no doubt that these two groups were paramilitaries fully backed by the Lankan government, these views put forward by Alston were deeply disappointing. We could not interpret these two views put forward by him as reflecting anything but the pro-Lankan position of the West.

Towards the end of 2005, I began visiting the Peace Secretariat regularly. My point of contact there was the media unit with which I had developed a working relationship in producing some video documentaries. The Peace Secretariat would also frequently ask me to do some translation of local news reports and editorials that appeared in the local daily *Eelanatham* or the Jaffna dailies *Uthayan* and *Eelanaadu*. These translations were uploaded onto the Peace Secretariat website for the benefit of the international community. These pieces often reflected views and news that failed to appear in any other English media.

I remember one particular editorial in the *Uthayan* newspaper in January 2006, which was forceful in its message. I therefore decided to translate it for the website. The editorial was on the southern—Sinhala and English—media. I liked it because it depicted the nature of the southern media forcefully by just using one incident in the parliament. When it was uploaded onto the website, the footnote to say that it was an *Uthayan* editorial was accidentally omitted. The international media picked up this website item as a statement from the LTTE and released news reports quoting this piece and highlighted the following paragraph where it said that the military campaign may have to be re-launched.

"It is certain that if the southern media continues in this

style of Sinhala chauvinism, the southern people will never understand the basic causes of the Tamils' just struggle. This means the Sinhala society immersed in chauvinistic thought and arrogant in its majoritarian attitude, is not going to allow a just solution to the Tamil problem. As a result, a peaceful resolution will become an unreachable dream and the Tamil side will be pushed into a situation of finding justice through military means."

The international media's appetite for LTTE statements on re-launching the military campaign was very transparent throughout this period. The mistake on the website was quickly fixed and no one was annoyed by it. I learned to be more careful with political messages that would go on the Peace Secretariat website.

I had never independently written any political message that went on the Peace Secretariat website. However, by early 2006, I gradually gained independence on deciding the content of all other material that would go on it. Looking back, I do not know of any specific decisions that were either conveyed to me or that I made on my own that led to this situation. I think the attraction of the excellent internet access had some role to play. The luring tactics of the head of the Peace Secretariat, Pulitheevan, may also have had something to do with it. In Vanni, I gained many friendships with young LTTE members. Karan was my first friend and Pulitheevan, alias Puli, became my next friend.

Because of the manner in which my role at the Peace Secretariat had evolved, I never thought that the role made me a member of the Peace Secretariat staff, who were otherwise all LTTE members. There were civilians employed there for cleaning, tea-making, and in its video and photography unit, but in the Peace Secretariat per se there were no civilians. Other expatriate volunteers came and went, but except for one more person, who stayed for one year, no one stayed longer than a few weeks. It was the members of the SLMM, the international peace monitors associated with the 2002 ceasefire process, who implicitly told me that I was indeed a member of the Peace Secretariat. There was some unease on my part at being thought of that way, but I quietly swallowed it because I enjoyed what I was doing. Thus by May 2006, I stopped doing work for NESoHR because it would be seen as a conflict of interest to work for both the Peace Secretariat and NESoHR. However, I returned to work for NESoHR after the assassination of Kili-father because the need at NESoHR was seen as very acute.

Once I started spending longer hours at the Peace Secretariat, I came into constant contact with SLMM staff whose writ included a daily visit to the Peace Secretariat—their contact point with the LTTE. It is after this shift in my role that I learnt more about the SLMM point system for counting violations of the ceasefire agreement by both sides. The point system implemented by the SLMM permitted anyone to submit complaints of violations of the ceasefire agreement against either party to the SLMM. The public contact points were its two liaison offices in Colombo and Vanni, and the six district offices in the Tamil homeland. In each of the six districts where the SLMM had district offices, it had also convened a local committee. These local committees consisted of the SLMM officers in the district plus two nominees each by the Peace Secretariats of both parties. These district committees would discuss the complaints that they had received and rule on them. SLMM regularly published Tamil Eelam-wide statistics on violations of the ceasefire agreement by both parties.

Though the aim of instituting this counting system may have been genuine, its implementation turned out to be so ridiculous that it was nothing but a comedy. The error was not entirely the SLMM's. The Lankan Military cleverly exploited its system to accrue points against the LTTE; while the LTTE, aka the Peace Secretariat, failed to match this level of exploitation of the point system. With the help of one Peace Secretariat member, I decided to up the ante and match the Lankan Military tactic. The largest number of ceasefire violations by the Lankan Military were taking place at sea, where attacks on fishermen were common. We collated these and sent piles of complaint letters to the SLMM. I am not sure whether it was due to this or otherwise, but soon after we started sending piles of complaints, the SLMM decided to scrap the point system because it failed to reflect the on-the-ground reality. The point counting of the SLMM had gone on from 2002 until mid-2006, and it need not have taken the SLMM to see that the counting was ridiculous and did not reflect reality on ground. Yet, it was allowed to continue as long as it did, as long as it was working in favor of the government. This bias was evident in other ways too.

After I left NESoHR, all the official meetings with Westerners that I was part of had to do with the child soldier issue, which I describe later. While at the Peace Secretariat, however, I had chances to listen, sitting in the adjacent room, to several meetings with Westerners. Thamilselvan shifted these meetings to a different, more secluded, location towards the end of 2006, and I lost this opportunity for listening in. These meetings perplexed me a great deal. I had never experienced meetings that involved diplomacy at this level. Never was I able to observe a convergence of positions during these meetings. The two sides seemed to always talk over each other's heads, as if they were maintaining positions for audiences not then present. Is this how diplomatic meetings always go? Or is it because of cultural differences, in which case do all meetings between Westerners and others end up like this? Or was this peculiar to the Vanni context, where the actual decisions for both sides were made elsewhere and these meetings were just sounding boards. Is it possible that this is also true for many other contexts of international diplomacy?

I was able to observe that the visiting team always held a document-instrument-mandate on which they would base their talk. It would be the ceasefire agreement or the Geneva Convention or Optional Protocol on Child Soldiers or some instrument somewhere about freedom of movement and so on. The visitors would always try to turn the discussion back to this specific instrument. The LTTE team, aka Thamilselvan and his interpreter, would talk about the long history of injustices to the Tamils, which seemed to test the patience of the visiting team. The visitors often had very little knowledge of the history of the "Tamil problem". Norwegian ambassadors and SLMM Heads had better knowledge of the "Tamil problem", but the communication was still problematic and the gaps were not narrowed by the meetings.

Yet these meetings would entail so much drama, consuming so many resources. The team would arrive by helicopter either in Kilinochchi or in Vavuniya. In the latter case, an LTTE convoy with some important leaders and LTTE police in vehicles and on motorbikes would meet them at Puliyankulam, and the convoy would race down to Kilinochchi on roads that were in poor condition. A large contingent of journalists—local, Colombo, and international—would have already arrived, waiting to report on the meeting. As the meeting progressed inside the Peace Secretariat or later in a more secluded location, the media contingent would wait under the shade of the mango trees at the Peace Secretariat, accepting its hospitality. They must have had a great time sitting in round-table formations and chatting for hours, waiting for the meeting to end. When the meeting finished, the visiting team would meet the media standing under the mango trees for a few minutes. Never did the visiting team give an in-depth media interview to the long awaiting troop of journalists. On the other hand, Thamilselvan would take the troop of journalists indoors to the media room of the Peace Secretariat and give them a long, often repeated, monotonous talk, none of which would be reported by any media other than the Vanni media. The exception was when Thamilselvan mentioned something about *"Colombo will be attacked in retaliation..."* or something similar, which would be carried as headlines in all other media. The differentiation could not be more stark.

One cries for justice and the other holds out "documents". One cries to the media to report the injustices and the media wants and waits for it to say "attack" so that it can report that. "Occidental mysticism" is how an Indian activist once described the compartmentalization of "justice" into instruments and institutions, and this was a solid example. At the end of it all, I would be given the audio file of Thamilselvan's media meeting to transcribe into English for uploading onto the website. It could be frustrating.

I was also closely associated with the documents produced by the Peace Secretariat during the last two direct peace talks in Geneva in 2006. With the help of Peace Secretariat staff, all working overtime, we produced several documents on human rights, High Security Zones, paramilitaries, children, women, and ceasefire violations for submission at the peace talks. The paramilitary document broke out as a media hit during the first Geneva talks. Most of the material in it was given to us by Marshall, alias Ilanthiraiyan, who was the LTTE military spokesperson. He in turn had collected it from various LTTE intelligence sources; the rest was collected by Peace Secretariat staff. However, it was the document on ceasefire violations that went through many versions at the instigation of Thamilselvan, who was never satisfied by the style in which it was written. The articles of the 2002 ceasefire agreement were dissected in great detail by many inside and outside Vanni with the aim of proving that one or the other party was responsible for seriously violating the 2002 ceasefire agreement clauses. The misleading SLMM counting of ceasefire violations, explained above, would form the basis of much of the analysis by those outside Vanni. Even today, there is no general agreement on who was the gravest violator of the ceasefire clauses, which goes to prove that both sides were equally culpable, which the peace makers could not or would not highlight in time to correct the flaws.

In my role as the person who did all the English drafting of letters and documents for Thamilselvan and the Peace Secretariat during 2006-2007, two instances were controversial and I will describe them here. I am not sure who did most of the English drafting prior to my presence, but Thamilselvan's interpreter was one of them.

One of the controversial letters was the second in a series of two letters sent in early 2006 to the SLMM Head objecting to the SLMM boarding the Lankan Navy ships for patrolling the sea. The 2002 ceasefire agreement had failed to demarcate areas of the sea where the LTTE could exercise, and this had caused a few serious incidents very early on in the ceasefire. When, in 2003, the SLMM Head of that time attempted to renegotiate a clause to resolve this issue, he was promptly packed away and replaced at the insistence of the Lankan government.[13] The issue of LTTE's right to use the sea had since remained unresolved but without incident, though harassment of fishermen by the Lankan Navy had continued. This harassment began to peak in 2006. There were numerous attacks on fishermen's boats and some had already disappeared.

The LTTE seemed to have decided to take action, and one move was to stop the SLMM boarding the Lankan Naval ships. A letter was sent to the SLMM Head in May 2006 urging him to stop the practice. He promptly replied to the effect that it must continue. A day or two later Pulitheevan stormed into my room and demanded that I draft another, stronger letter to the head of SLMM demanding an immediate halt to the SLMM boarding Lankan Naval ships. The letter said something to the effect that this is the last warning and that the Lankan Naval ships may be attacked, even if an SLMM officer had boarded it. I think an LTTE ship was already on its way to attack a Lankan Naval convoy which was transporting Navy personnel. The letter Pulitheevan demanded was meant to ameliorate any fallout. The LTTE was angry that the SLMM was providing an escort for Lankan naval personnel who were attacking and disappearing Tamil fishermen, while a similar escort was not available to them. The strong message from LTTE in the second letter must have ruffled some feathers in Western circles. One SLMM member apparently said that this letter was one of the two reasons for the proscription of LTTE by the European Union (EU) soon after. The other reason stated by the SLMM officer for the proscription by the EU was the assassination of the Lankan Foreign Minister, Kadirgamar, in 2005.

Later on, in July 2006, when an LTTE delegation was in Oslo, an LTTE member with close connections to the LTTE Naval wing described to me exactly what had happened during that sea episode. Apparently, the Lankan Navy convoy was transporting Navy personnel from Jaffna to the south for their holiday break escorted by a Lankan Naval patrol boat with an SLMM officer on it. The LTTE attack resulted in the death of Navy personnel and put the SLMM officer in danger. We together wrote a two page document, giving maps and other details of the incident, and sent it to Oslo.

The other controversial document that I translated was for Thamilselvan. It was an email interview for major media to coincide with a Tokyo Co-Chairs meeting held in September 2006 to discuss the peace process. The original interview answers were drafted in Tamil by Thamilselvan and it was a standard letter to bring media attention to some of the issues the LTTE wanted to highlight. While I was translating it, Pulitheevan suddenly said to add a sentence to the effect that the LTTE was ready for peace talks. This was after the first Geneva talks and there was no clear expectation that there would be another round of talks, though the Co-Chairs were pushing for it. The email interview was sent and as Pulitheevan expected, it caught the media's attention and was reported positively. However, seeing the unexpected sentence in his interview, an angry Thamilselvan came to the Peace Secretariat that night. Pulitheevan and I had to explain the misdeed to him. We all went home and later that night Pulitheevan arrived at my residence with a bag full of *naaval* plums, my favorite, and we talked about all sorts of things till midnight eating the *naaval* plums. He was clearly upset and felt bad that he had put me also on the spot. A few days later he said that Thamilselvan had congratulated him for that clever media stunt. The October 2006 Geneva peace talks came after this episode and were the last direct talks held between the two parties.

Thus, for a brief period, I was a spectator in a second-class seat to the drama of the peace process. Perhaps at times I was also a peripheral actor who was inadvertently drawn into some controversies.

I would like to conclude this chapter with a little note on the uniquely delicious, tiny, purple *naaval* plums. I have many childhood memories of them. There was one of these fruit trees just behind my bedroom in Jaffna which offered the seasonal *naaval* plums—and also some snakes hiding in its holes, and some ghosts that peeked at night through my bedroom window. At the Peace Secretariat, it became well known that they were my favorite fruit. Even Thamilselvan would send me a one liter bottle filled with the best variety that was only available in Poonahari, the favorite haunt of his team. My mouth waters thinking about it. On the day of his death, I went to his home which was full of mourners. On seeing me, the people at the home cried out saying that he had told them just the previous day to send some *naaval* plums to me.

9

Child soldiers

Older members of the LTTE told me that in the 1980s, to promote its image, LTTE placed advertisements in Tamil newspapers with very young child recruits in LTTE fatigues. Taking in neglected children, putting them through an education and turning them into a *poorali*, a respected member of society, was seen by the LTTE as a positive act. In due course this deteriorated into a practice of recruitment of 14 to 17-year-olds, and sometimes even younger children, through intense propaganda. One such member I came to know well was a leading member of the LTTE Peace Secretariat, Bavan, who joined in 1993 as a fourteen-year-old and lost one leg in battle in 1995. Following recovery from his injury, he was educated in IT and English for the next six years, and became a leading member of the Peace Secretariat.

During the evolution of this LTTE culture in the 1980s, the main international instrument on the age of recruitment, the Geneva Convention, restricted the age of recruitment to fifteen. There was no UN agenda or instruments on child soldiers. Indeed the UN Convention on the Rights of the Child was declared only in 1987, which also only specified fifteen as the age limit for recruitment. The child soldier phenomenon within LTTE was thus part of its growth at a time when there was no international agenda on child soldiers. It was only in the late 1990s that the high-profile campaign by the UN and international NGOs on child soldiers was launched. In 1998, the UN's Special Representative on Children in Armed Conflict, Olara Otunnu, visited Vanni and supposedly extracted a promise from the LTTE that they would not recruit anyone under the age of seventeen. The child soldier phenomenon within the LTTE as known in the international circles was thus born. LTTE had always denied that they made such a promise to Olara Otunnu.

As a result of these two staggered developments, the LTTE child soldier phenomenon, as it was known after the late 1990s, was a process of contradiction between these two developments, the internal cultural dimension and the external campaign dimension. LTTE leadership, many of whom were child soldiers themselves and were immersed in the cultural process, saw no rights violation. One instance that made me realize this was during the only conversation I ever had with the two top LTTE female military leaders, Thurka and Vithusha. Vithusha, on learning that I was involved with the child soldier issue, said in a wounded but exasperated tone how they had been ordered to release all those born in 1990 and after, who at that time would have been under seventeen years of age. These LTTE leaders judged the external campaign as vindictive and tried to manage it rather than eliminate the practice of child soldiers. The blockade of the area under LTTE control aided this management to some degree.

The child soldier issue had perplexed many Tamil Diaspora activists including myself. Because of the ferocity of the international campaign to the exclusion of all other child rights issues, we tended to blame the international agencies for exaggerating the problem as a means of demonizing LTTE. When I arrived in Vanni with this background, the child soldier issue remained a black box to me, even though it was discussed widely among Diaspora activists who were visiting Vanni in large numbers. In 2005, discussing the issue with a few LTTE members to whom I had limited access at that time, three categories of push and pull forces on the children to join the LTTE became obvious. These were economic, war-related, and cultural factors. It was not to be the task of UNICEF or the other international agencies to acknowledge these push and pull factors that created the child soldiers. Garca Machel's 1996 global report was perhaps the first of its kind to come out and describe the interconnectedness of all these issues. Despite this, the campaigners carried on as if recruiting under-18-year-olds was the most serious crime against humanity. When a UN official privately described the child soldier issue as a sexy issue for the media, I thought it put much of the hype in context.

After the ceasefire, the pressure on LTTE mounted to eliminate this practice. Its Tamil supporters became frustrated because the LTTE kept claiming that it had released all the child soldiers and had stopped recruiting them. But UNICEF kept producing more and more instances of new child recruitment. As proof of its cessation, the LTTE did release hundreds of child soldiers, first through the 2003 Action Plan with UNICEF and then through NESoHR. However, UNICEF, which was mandated by the UN Security Council to monitor the issue in Sri Lanka, kept reporting new cases. Families who were now well aware of the work of UNICEF eagerly kept UNICEF updated of new instances.

After the arrival of the SLMM as part of the 2002 ceasefire, the child soldier issue took on another dimension when the ceasefire monitors, the SLMM, decided to accept complaints of child soldier recruitment also as a ceasefire violation. Indeed a large percentage of the ceasefire violations against the LTTE counted by SLMM were of child soldier recruitment. The debate on whether this counting justified and strengthened the ceasefire agreement continued long after. The child soldier issue, however, had now become of enormous importance to the LTTE.

NESoHR, too, was taking complaints from the parents and advocating for the release of children. The process was only 50 percent successful, and at the time I did not understand why this was the case. As a newcomer to Vanni, I was not let into the discussions that would have brought out the reasons. Some people at NESoHR thought that writing life stories about child soldiers based on the narratives by child soldiers themselves would bring out the true picture. Before I could seriously adopt this approach, I left NESoHR. In hindsight, I do not think this approach would have worked given the international stance on the issue.

At NESoHR the child soldier issue was mainly Kili-father's domain, though I kept following the proceedings. For the most part, the picture that developed from my children's homes experience and what I saw at NESoHR fitted well. Most of the children who were being released were children affected badly by the war. However, I also realized that I did not really understand the child soldier issue, which now appeared to be a lot more complex than I originally thought. I met boys who were left as child servants at other people's houses, who then ran away to join the LTTE. I met girls who ran away from well-to-do families and professed that they wanted to fight for their country. It was obvious that they were running away from something in their lives. There were parents grieving the loss of their child who had gone into the LTTE fold, but were ignorant of the reasons that pushed them.

During this time at NESoHR, I happened to attend for the very first time a meeting on child soldiers headed by Thamilselvan. Many other civilian community leaders who had done some work with children were also in attendance. This meeting, intended as a launching pad for the Child Protection Authority (CPA), did not go anywhere. I, however, for the first time heard directly from Thamilselvan about the seriousness with which the LTTE intended to implement the minimum age policy of seventeen. I was even more confounded as to why it was so difficult to implement this policy.

It was after I left NESoHR and started working at Peace Secretariat that I had the opportunity to hear directly from many LTTE members. Things now started to become clearer to me. I noticed the noncommittal stance of some members towards the minimum age and the take-it-easy approach of some others towards this issue. The whole concept seemed alien and meaningless to LTTE members, and I was able to see that this derived from an institutional culture with two decades of history. It was a culture that predated the 2001 Optional Protocol on Children in Armed Conflict, a culture born of decades of actual experience of war. It was only in this 2001 Protocol that the age limit was set at eighteen for the first time, and that, too, only for non-state armed actors; states were permitted to recruit those under 18. This is a major point that has been missed in the media hype.

Around the middle of 2006 I felt I had something worthwhile to say about this issue. I also felt that ideally it was best said by the LTTE itself. I wrote up a report for LTTE with no hope that it would be published as an LTTE report. To my surprise Thamilselvan liked it and with some modifications, more on the style of writing than the content, it was published in August 2006[14] and was well received.

The pressure on the LTTE grew to a very high pitch, though its no-nonsense implementation did not start until after the visit in 2006 by Alan Rock, Special Envoy of the UN Special Representative for Children in Armed Conflict. When Alan Rock's visit took place towards the end of 2006, I was suddenly told by Pulitheevan that I was now the Director of the Child Protection Authority and I should head its meeting with Alan Rock. My role as part of this body in monitoring the child soldier issue and liaising with UNICEF on the same issue began with this meeting.

Following Alan Rock's visit, efforts were made by Thamilselvan to strengthen the Child Protection Authority by creating a document for its mandate and also increasing its civilian membership. UNICEF, too, urged the LTTE to strengthen the resources available to this body. Yet in reality these efforts did not have much substance as it related to addressing the actual problem—as opposed to its entrenchment as an international issue, and this body failed to go past handling the issue of child soldiers.

Once Pulitheevan asked me to take on the role of Director of this body, I knew that I was not going to lie back and accept the LTTE's softly-softly approach on the issue of child soldiers. I suspect the LTTE fraternity knew it too. In this role I worked with LTTE's liaison office, which was physically located adjacent to the Peace Secretariat, for liaising with international agencies. For more than one year, I had weekly meetings with UNICEF to discuss progress.

I had disagreements with both sides, the LTTE and UNICEF, and on some occasions I broke down and cried. Once it was because of the "mandate mentality" of UNICEF that displayed insensitivity to the plight of some children, mainly the girls. Once it was because of an LTTE action that ignored my "authority" in this area. For one year, all of 2007, this was my primary goal, ensuring that the LTTE did not fall back into the old softly-softly approach. It consumed me. I saw a clear demonstration of the no-nonsense approach of LTTE when I heard of middle-level LTTE leaders given punishment for recruiting children. It was mainly kitchen-duty punishment, which was a common form of mild punishment given to members. But when it was given to a leader, it was viewed as serious punishment and talked about. A senior female LTTE leader told me that when those under her recruited someone even a month younger than the specified age, her stomach churned in fear of punishment.

Towards the end of 2006 and all of 2007, LTTE was implementing the policy to not take anyone born in 1990 and after, which effectively was a policy of not taking anyone under the age of seventeen. It was during this phase that I began closely monitoring the release of child soldiers. It was clear that the leadership of the LTTE was keen on implementing the release of all child soldiers under the age of seventeen, whether a complaint was lodged with UNICEF or not. But gaining the full cooperation of field members of the LTTE took time.

Thamilselvan was determined and I knew it. I had direct access to him to complain about lapses. I began supplying regular updates to Thamilselvan about releases and new recruitment; something that until then was not given to him. I think it also helped in pushing for much stronger actions to end it. He called regular meetings and conveyed his concerns and displeasure for not speeding up the project. I pushed for a notice in the local media to call for complaints about under-seventeen recruitment, and this became well known among the public. LTTE members who defied the policy were now punished and the culture reluctantly began to change. The LTTE kept trying to maintain the right to recruit seventeen-year-olds, citing the extensive social services it provided and claiming its defacto-state status. However, by the beginning of 2008, the LTTE relented, adhering to the policy of a minimum age of eighteen.

There were many legitimate hiccups in implementing the project. We were all frustrated when both UNICEF and the international media were uncompromising in slapping the label of child recruiters on the LTTE, despite the massive efforts that were underway. Their excuse was that the LTTE had made similar promises before but failed to carry them through. The LTTE on the other hand said it never made a promise to not recruit below the age of eighteen.

The efforts to end the child soldier problem within the LTTE involved ending new recruitment and releasing those within the ranks. Thamilselvan told me that he would take responsibility to end recruitment, and he was very successful in this, although it took a few months after Alan Rock's visit to achieve this one hundred percent. The other side of the effort, to release those within the ranks, took more effort and time. The early success came in the Vanni area that was administered by the LTTE.

We came across several names of extremely young children from Batticaloa and Amparai in the UNICEF list of LTTE child soldiers. We eventually traced these children in Senchoolai and Arivuchchoolai children's home. LTTE had taken these children, who were not receiving adequate care, into the branch of Senchoolai that was started in Batticaloa following the 2004 tsunami. When the LTTE withdrew from Batticaloa, these children were shifted to the Vanni Senchoolai and Arivuchchoolai. UNICEF refused to remove their names from the list, insisting that they would do so only after they were reunited with their families. But neither UNICEF nor ICRC were able to complete that task. In some cases they could not trace the families who had been displaced or gone missing following the tsunami. Even in cases where the families were traced, the Lankan government refused permission to take the children from Vanni to the eastern districts. Thus it remained that even at this time, and despite the latest LTTE efforts, the youngest child in the LTTE was only seven years old. In fact, even in late 2007, there were international media reports, quoting UNICEF, that the youngest person in the LTTE was only seven years old. When I confronted the head of UNICEF Sri Lanka at that time about this report, the comment was that UNICEF could not do anything about it because it still was a "fact". The media kept reporting this "fact", a sexy issue, and UNICEF "could do nothing" about it, though they were fully aware of the background to the "seven-year-old LTTE member".

There were many more instances of misreporting by the media that convinced me of the unhealthy and biased media attraction to this issue, which was acknowledged privately to me by more than one UNICEF official. Some cases will illustrate my point. A nine-year-old girl with a mild intellectual handicap, who was abused at home, began behaving erratically at school. One day she was found hanging around in her class room late at night to avoid going home. An LTTE member eventually removed her from school and put her in the care of a children's home. Someone, probably a family member, reported this to UNICEF. This child remained in the children's home even in early 2009 because she did not have a safe home to go to. Yet, she remained as a child soldier entry in the UNICEF database though UNICEF eventually removed her from their database.

A seventeen-year-old truck driver employed by the finance division of the LTTE was killed by a Lankan claymore in 2007. UNICEF reported it as a child soldier killed in action. I met his family after his death. He was the eldest, and the sole breadwinner of his family with three younger siblings and his mother. For this reason, LTTE officially made him a member of the auxiliary force, killed while on duty, so that his family could continue to receive the stipulated income from the LTTE. This had prompted a UNICEF child soldier accusation. We made a detailed report of this case on the Peace Secretariat website.

Again in April 2007, an Associated Press (AP) report quoting UNICEF said that LTTE had recruited many child soldiers over the last month in Batticaloa. It was a time when I personally received all cases of child soldier recruitment from UNICEF on a weekly basis. There were hardly any such cases from Batticaloa reported to me by UNICEF. Either a UNICEF official or the AP reporter was lying. Again, we wrote a detailed report about this on the Peace Secretariat website.

There was a highly negative article in the New Zealand *Herald* in late 2007, written by UNICEF New Zealand, about LTTE and child soldiers. It was completely against the grain of developments at that time, and attempted to portray this issue in a very negative light. I raised this with UNICEF at that time and they tried to distance themselves from the article saying UNICEF in New Zealand and other developed countries were independent bodies whose main task was to raise funds. It was obvious that the child soldier issue within the LTTE was sexy and a great fundraiser.

By the end of 2007, the age limit for recruitment for LTTE had been set at eighteen, and UNICEF and the international media had begun to grudgingly acknowledge the efforts of the LTTE. I wrote regular reports for CPA, including a table challenging the UNICEF database on LTTE child soldiers. This was regularly published on the LTTE Peace Secretariat website. The latest of these tables is shown below. This UNICEF database served a tool used by the international community to constantly discredit the LTTE on this issue.

In my view it was Thamilselvan who spearheaded the program to end the child soldier problem and also implemented the one person per family recruitment policy. He had the entire recruitment process under his control, thus under the political wing. Following his death in late 2007, we started receiving some complaints of underage recruitment by other LTTE divisions, and this was beginning to be a headache because we now did not have an easy tracing mechanism to locate the child and the culprit, nor also the single point of contact to make complaints. The withdrawal of UNICEF, together with other international agencies in late 2008, enraged many LTTE members. Arguments were repeatedly put forward, challenging the UNICEF campaigning on child soldiers when it could abandon the entire population of children to the impending genocide. We fought against this thinking and the new head of the political wing, Nadeesan, gave support to us. The CPA effort continued even after the departure of UNICEF, but the frequent aerial bombing also interrupted our work. Following the Kilinochchi evacuation in late 2008, I could not be active in this area and as far as I know the work of CPA was very much weakened.

This experience with CPA was most valuable for me for several reasons. I was permitted to discuss recruitment issues in detail with LTTE members because of my role in it. I met and learned more about the families and their issues with the children who were with the LTTE, and there were scores of different facets to it. I learned about the problems with single mandate campaigns, such as the one carried out by the international community with respect to this issue. Single mandate campaigns permit one to select an issue and drive at full throttle, disregarding all other interrelated issues. It simplifies the otherwise complex human existence on which it is difficult to drive a campaign. Single mandate campaigns also give legitimacy to unjust campaigns if one elects to abuse them to demonize something. In the case of this issue with the LTTE, many international groups claimed that a change of heart from the LTTE came about because of such a full throttle campaign. But it was also unjust because an instantaneous change of an established culture was demanded. The international campaign also failed to take into account that during the period when this culture evolved there was no international discourse condemning this practice.

Snapshot of UNICEF underage database as at end of May 2008 of recruitment prior to 2008	Amparai	Batticaloa	Jaffna	Trinco	Vanni	Vavuniya	Total
Totals:	20	53	6	14	17	15	125
Category-1 Based on information provided by UNICEF in the past, CPA speculates that these 27 children, who were released prior to 2008, were not verified due to prevailing security concerns for UNICEF staff and displacement of the families concerned.	1	1	1	1	15	8	27
Category-2 These 6 children who have always been cared for in the children's home continue to be in the UNICEF database and they too face the same plight as those in category-3.	5	1					6
Category-3: Another 27 children have been identified by the CPA but remain in the UNICEF list because of the prevailing situation is preventing them from being united with their families despite the efforts being made by the ICRC and UNICEF.	6	17	2	2			27
Category-4 includes two persons who are indeed older than the age given by UNICEF.					2		2
Category-5: There remain a further 63 children whom CPA has not traced within the LTTE. UNICEF has not provided CPA with the additional information that was sought to trace these children. 53 of these children are from the eastern districts of Amparai, Batticaloa and Trincomalee. CPA strongly suspects that a large percentage of these 63 children are indeed not with the LTTE.	8	34	3	11		7	63
Category-6: No advocacy cases: In addition to the above five categories, UNICEF numbers also include few cases of underage recruitment whose families allegedly do not want advocacy with the LTTE. This number presently stands at 7.							

10

Debates on society

The LTTE community, as to be expected, was constantly engaged in debates on social justice issues. Their debates were not just theoretical like the debates one finds in most parts of the world. They were engaged with the immediate need to implement a policy. These debates were thus more genuine, serious, and enthusiastic. That a division of LTTE was continuously upgrading and creating a body of law for the society it was building, further enriched this debating society. The legal experts in Vanni were still mostly amateurs, despite the fact that the Tamil community as a whole was endowed with experts who had a great knowledge on traditional and modern law. These experts by and large were absent from Vanni. Yet it was possible to have meaningful debates because the society and governance was relatively simple and the debates were idealistic.

Some members enjoyed this debating aspect of their life and contributed more than the others. I can remember either hearing or being part of many debates on child soldiers, media freedom, cricket, women's rights and the division of labor within family, pure Tamil names for babies, traditional attire, nuances in translations, spin doctoring, forced recruitment, protection of women in law, and many more. I have addressed the debates on child soldiers and women in separate chapters. I will deal with the rest here.

While working at NESoHR, one had the opportunity to see the civilian side of the society and all the pain and suffering they were facing. Its employees were mostly young civilians in their early twenties who had grown up with the war and all the limitations it had placed on their development. Yet they were still capable young people, who understood the role of NESoHR in their society. Yet I had not heard them engage in intellectual debate. There was a foundation committee for NESoHR made up of community leaders which formulated its direction. This committee, however, met only a handful of times because the members were from all over Tamil Eelam. Even these occasional meetings could not take place after mid-2006 when the A9 road was closed. These committee meetings did not engage in lively debates. It was only after I had begun to work at the LTTE Peace Secretariat that I interacted extensively with LTTE members and heard and took part in debates with them. I did notice that those who worked at and visited the Peace Secretariat were of a specific kind. They were better read, had a higher level of education, and were even better in their command of English.

It must be said here, however, that among the activities that all LTTE members, both men and women, enjoyed most was reminiscing about events of the past. Watching them enjoying such conversations, one would think that they were the happiest people on earth because the interactions would be filled with laughter. They would discuss dead comrades, past battles, instances of near capture by the Lankan Military, receiving punishment from superiors, etc. But all of these subjects were discussed with a sense of humor. One SLMM member, who had noticed this without being able to understand the language, once commented that for a set of liberation fighters they did spend an awful lot of time talking and laughing. All of them indeed carried with them a great deal of painful memories and this, it seemed, was their therapy.

In 2007 Sri Lanka was in the Cricket World Cup finals. Noting the enthusiasm of Tamils, including some members of the LTTE, in the Cricket World Cup, Colombo and Western media began speculating that cricket could be a unifying issue for Tamils and Sinhalese. Many of us thought and said, with a touch of sarcasm, that this was what this same media said about the 2004 tsunami. Interestingly the Cricket World Cup created quite a lively debate at the Peace Secretariat as well. Strangely, I heard comments from some male LTTE members that there was nothing wrong in being an LTTE member and also supporting the Lankan cricket team in the World Cup. It was even said that sports and politics should not mix. I had heard an earful of this while living in New Zealand in 1981 during the anti-apartheid protests against the South African Springbok rugby tour. This debate in New Zealand, on politics and sports had already set a world standard for the relationship between the two. Indeed the sports boycott of South Africa was given much credit for ending apartheid there. For LTTE members this was news. Yet all of the female LTTE members whom I knew and the majority of the male LTTE members did not support the Lankan cricket team. However, the ardent supporters of the Lankan cricket team were also some of the most loyal LTTE members. This male psychology in regard to cricket puzzled me and the others. I suspect this puzzle persists even today among some male Tamil civilians who are ardent supporters of both an independent Tamil Eelam and the Lankan cricket team.

For Marshall, alias Ilanthirayan, the LTTE military spokesperson, the cricket issue was a non-topic for debate. Sometime in 2006, Marshal was given an office in the Peace Secretariat building from where he carried out his duties as the military spokesperson. Marshal was highly intelligent and creative. He always came up with new ideas. Even in late 2008, when things were looking very bleak, he talked about new types of projects for the survival of the people. He had turned his interest to small-scale renewable production of fuel as a practical solution to the prevailing acute fuel shortage caused by the Lankan embargo. As always, Marshall directed his energy on too many different subjects and thus never persevered with his ideas to completion. Perhaps, if he had had able assistants, he would have made a greater mark. Marshall was from Batticaloa, and he was educated at St Michael's College up to GCE-A/L when he quit school to join the LTTE. He never tired of describing his life working on his family land, where he had grown up doing all kinds of work. He had great appreciation for the environment and the wildlife, and he was a treasure trove of knowledge. One of his theories, to which I too subscribe, is that during the 80s and 90s the young men and women who joined the LTTE were also the most responsible sons and daughters of their families, those who cared most among the siblings about their family. Marshall was a man of many trades. He had worked as a barman in a hotel in Colombo, and he had lassoed cows on his family land. Within the LTTE, he had translated books, and had been the political head for Batticaloa before becoming the military spokesperson. He was also a music composer. His style of writing was entertaining and insightful, but he never wrote much due to his lack of application.

Marshall was also a member of the CPA and accompanied me to many of the meetings with UNICEF on child soldiers. As a strategy to balance the incessant UNICEF campaign on child soldiers, he suggested highlighting the Lankan bombing raids that were terrorizing the children especially during school hours. He demanded that UNICEF fund a project to paint the roofs of all the schools as clearly identifiable, which was implemented later by UNICEF. He also asked UNICEF to demand that the Lankan bombing raids be not carried out during school hours. In this he was not successful.

Puli, the head of the Peace Secretariat, was quite a different personality. His jovial nature gave him his own brand of diplomatic style. He had made many friends in Colombo during the early phase of the 2002 ceasefire using his style of diplomacy. As far as I could see, he was a good administrator, though not all would agree on this. Unlike almost all the members whom I came to know well, who had either been child soldiers or had joined immediately after their GCE-A/L examination, Puli was older. He was in his early twenties when he joined LTTE and was pursuing a course in mathematics at Jaffna University, which he did not complete. In fact, one member who was at the initiation camp for new recruits with Puli said to me when they saw Puli at the camp, that they all thought: what was such an old man doing there? Puli's commitment to Tamil Eelam and his belief that it was achievable were probably stronger than that of many other members. At least philosophically, Puli empathized with women's equality and was quick to understand the difficulties faced by girls in the offices. He had discussed with me on many occasions approaches to easing the domestic duties that weighed down on the women and prevented them from more active public roles. He came up with various ideas, which included some form of communal facilities to replace the kitchen in the home. He was against the high degree of separation of men and women within the movement and believed that it was holding back the women.

Indeed both Marshall and Puli exhibited strong sympathies for women's issues, but the extent to which they were able to practice it in their family life was limited by the work demands placed on them. I had visited their family homes many times, and their family lives were cozy and joyous.

After mid-2006, the members who were part of the LTTE Peace Secretariat had regular translation duties, mostly translating the major articles in the English media about the peace process. Marshall's knowledge and experience in translation between Tamil and English was often the starting point of many interesting topics of discussion at the Peace Secretariat. Though Marshall's failure to apply his talent fully was regretted by some, it was always such a pleasure to hold a conversation with him because of his wide experience and his non-Jaffna origin, none of which I shared. The last time I met Marshall in Mullivaikaal was in March 2009. He offered me some books to read because we were all stuck in our tents listening to the shells whistling past. When I told him that I had decided to leave by ICRC ship, I could detect his disappointment and it made me feel guilty. Marshall is among those who remain missing after capture by the Lankan Military as they walked out of the war zone during the end war 2009.

A very senior LTTE member in his sixties, Thamileenthi-appa, as he was respectfully called, was well known in Vanni for his drive to eliminate foreign words in Tamil usage. There were many jokes circulating in Vanni about his style of creating brand new pure Tamil words for the more modern technology-related terms. Part of this drive by Thamileenthi-appa was to give pure Tamil names to newborns. He offered rewards for those who gave pure Tamil names to their newborns, and even promised rewards to those parents who would change the names of their older children to pure Tamil names. In Vanni, it was common to give names of *maaveerar* to babies, and many of the names of *maaveerar* like Milton, Castro, and Charles Anthony were not Tamil names. It was not surprising that Thamileenthi-appa's drive offended these parents, and it was hotly debated. His long years of driving for language purity had caught up with the entire population, and people indeed used very pure Tamil in Vanni. When I met my relatives living outside Vanni, they remarked about the quality of my Tamil speech resulting from my time in Vanni. Such was the effect of Thamileenthi-appa's drive for pure Tamil. At his insistence, Thamileenthi-appa, too, was on the battlelines, and he was killed by shelling in Mullivaikaal in 2009.

Around mid-2006, I was asked to teach English to Thuvaarakaa, daughter of Pirapaaharan, and Piriyatharshini, daughter of Nadeesan, who was the Head of Police at that time. The lessons were held at night and were given close to where I lived. Some precautions were taken so that it did not become public knowledge. At times Thuvaarakaa's mother, Mathivathani, would also accompany them. Thuvaarakaa was very intelligent and loved to chat about many things, and as a result we did very little English teaching and learning. Piriyatharshini was a very quiet girl. Thuvaarakaa was intrigued by the superstitions held by the Tamil people. During our conversations, I also learned of the secluded life Thuvaarakaa was forced to live for security reasons, which had denied her many of the things other children, both rich and poor, take for granted. For example Thuvaarakaa never had a chance to play a team sport like netball with the other children. She asked me eagerly about the game. Both girls were missing after May 2009, though they had been sighted around that time in Mullivaikaal.

From about the beginning of 2006 until the end of 2006, the entire Political Wing would meet at some place, which they referred to as an "*Erimalai* meeting". Thamilselvan would address this gathering, and the theme of these meetings was recruitment. About this time, many of the LTTE members in the political wing, whom I knew, were put on *parappurai* (propaganda) duty, a euphemism for the recruitment drive. At the Peace Secretariat there would be frequent discussions on the experiences of carrying out this duty. The duty at that time involved standing on the streets, stopping young people and talking to them about why they should join the LTTE. The general theme that I heard was that the young people, having become used to living without war, were in no mood to join the LTTE. During this time the media would carry stories of young people who had joined and why they had joined. There were at times large-scale joining of the young and the old, but mostly the old. This phase was deemed not successful enough to meet the demand for cadres. At some point past mid-2006, the strict enforcement of one member per family began.

The discussions and debates shifted with the forced recruitment. Only children, married men, and married women were initially exempt from the strict implementation forcing one member from each family to .

become a member of the LTTE. There were special cases that deserved exemption, and these were intensely debated. Exemption for UN employees and their family members, national employees of international agencies, state employees, and medical workers all came under discussion. The LTTE eventually granted exemption to UN employees, but refused to include their family members. International agencies failed in their efforts to gain exemption for their national employees.

The strict enforcement of the one per family policy affected the entire social fabric. It was a painful exercise for many LTTE members I knew. Indeed, it was a dilemma that affected all of us deeply, both civilians and the members. My moral self sat uncomfortably with this because my two children were outside this painful debate as they were living outside the island. Many parents were involved in hiding their children, while most were dealing with an emotional struggle of being part of a freedom movement practicing forced recruitment. Some parents went to extreme lengths to avoid their children being recruited, and the LTTE too went to extreme lengths to strictly implement this policy. The various tricks adopted by families and the LTTE would fill a book. Some of the LTTE tactics have been published, but none of the civilian tactics have appeared publicly.

The policy brought many contradictions to the social scene. Some parents wanted their younger child who was underage to join the LTTE, rather than recruit the older one for different reasons. Initially the LTTE did not include married people into their compulsory recruitment which in turn forced many hurried and very young marriages. Eventually those who married without LTTE permission after some date in 2006 were included in the target category for recruitment. I also heard the calculation, though I cannot remember the exact figures, that a large percentage of families in Vanni would not be affected by this policy because at least one member from these families was already either a member or a *maaveerar*. The policy had been implemented with the full knowledge that the majority would support it for this reason. Given that the LTTE was strictly and fairly adhering to the age limit of eighteen, the society came around to accepting this rule. Eventually, it appeared that the process was almost complete by the end of 2007 and some equilibrium had come about. I was taken aback when in late 2007 a mother of an underage recruit who came to seek his release from LTTE said without any hesitation that it was their duty to give one child for the freedom of the country.

Forced recruitment may not have been included in the international instruments, yet it was morally ambiguous. I know many LTTE members felt discomfort at being part of this. One justification and moral consolation that people found in this debate on forced recruitment was that it had been practiced by many countries during World War II, and that if the Western countries were under threat, then the Tamils were under even greater threat.

11

Women's liberation Vanni-style

Many younger civilian Tamil women idealize the military role of LTTE women because that was the most common depiction of LTTE women in LTTE literature. Militarism permitted many liberating characteristics for women. The training improved their demeanour that was otherwise conditioned by a culture that demanded a strictly subordinate role. Participation in battles raised their status to that of the LTTE men in the eyes of the general population. It gave them the freedom to act in the public space in ways that were not acceptable for the civilian woman. LTTE women were clearly different from the rest of the women. This, however, had a flow on effect for the civilian women too. There were many non-military areas in which the Vanni society exhibited greater pro-women character than the wider Tamil society. That is what I will try to show here.

When I initially entertained the idea of working in Vanni, I had hoped that I would be working on women's issues. I had no idea how I would enter this field because I had no contact with anyone who did this type of work in Vanni. Throughout my work at NESoHR and the Peace Secretariat, I kept looking for avenues for entering this field. I mentioned this to Pulitheevan on a few occasions and his response was always to say that I was free to use the Peace Secretariat resources to do women-related work. The problem was, until late 2008, I did not have the one basic resource, my time, which was eaten up by demands for writing reports. This delay was useful in that it allowed me to study the field.

I was able to see at close quarters that the peace talks that unfolded during this period did not have genuine female representation on either side. At the same time, both sides made it a point to include token gestures towards female representation. The one exception to this was LTTE Human Rights spokesperson, Selvi, but her role was limited to being a spokesperson only.

I also observed female members in their relationships with each other, with male members, and with the society at large, and the views they held on women both in the movement and in the wider community, etc. I also learned more about the organizations that specifically devoted their time to women's issues. Various aspects of women's issues kept coming up in different contexts—in private conversations, in the work I did, and in the problems I had to deal with in respect to female employees and members. Initially I was disappointed. I arrived in Vanni hoping for a more liberated enlightened womenfolk, both members and civilians, but failed to find it. Gradually I realized that my disappointment was the result of looking for signs of women's liberation through the glasses of Western feminist ideologies.

Though I did not have the statistics, just observing the number of women on the streets during peak hours dressed for work, it was obvious that a greater percentage of women in Vanni went to work outside the home. There were also more women in civilian clothes riding motorbikes on Vanni roads compared to the rest of the island. Women, both LTTE members as well as civilians, occupied the public space in large numbers. They were very visible on the roads and in the LTTE institutions. This gave Vanni a uniquely pro-woman character, which was absent elsewhere on the island.

In Vanni there were several institutions under the women's section of the political division of LTTE working to improve the women's condition. Two notable ones were the Women's Research Centre (CWR) and the Centre for Women's Development and Rehabilitation (CWDR). CWR published a magazine called *Nattru* (*Seedling*) which carried some good articles. Its circulation was limited, and the institution itself did not have a large public presence. CWDR on the other hand, due to the growing need for assistance for destitute women, had a larger presence and was in fact a rather large institution.

The LTTE police force and its associated courts, made up mostly of civilians, was a mixed-gender institution that was well represented by females. The police force, as well as the lawyers and the judges, had nearly 50 percent female members. This was quite an achievement. Even the laws enacted by the LTTE to be implemented by its courts had a gender equality that was absent in the Lankan laws. Lankan laws had remnants of older customary laws of the land. Indeed LTTE laws had some unique features that went overboard to protect women who may have been cheated by men with the promise of marriage. During my stay, I heard LTTE women arguing against this special provision in the law for females, saying women did not need special protection against being cheated by men. I viewed it as a sign of an already existing sense of empowerment of the women to assert that they did not need gender specific laws to protect them, and the law should be enacted and applied equally to both genders.

LTTE women, women employed by the LTTE institutions, and self employed women were all interconnected through the many LTTE institutions, resulting in a unique female culture. These women openly and routinely discussed domestic violence and other problems faced by women. They were all on the lookout for women who needed a helping hand. Several LTTE institutions including health, welfare, banking-development, police, law, and the media supported this female culture by providing supporting services. These institutions all had more than 50 percent female representation. Some of them were run solely by women, both LTTE and civilian, and for civilian women. Women needing help were directed to the appropriate institutions, which were all focused on giving a helping hand to women. This was the best feature of this female culture—the elimination of destitution through universal women's action. It was a unique kind of feminism, created by connecting the majority of women living all over Vanni, from all walks of life, for public action regarding women and children in need of help.

"Why did I join?"

In my involvement with women's groups in Vanni, I met a category of civilian women whose family support structures were broken mainly due to the war. It was easy to think that the young among them would be prime targets for recruitment by the LTTE. Though this was partly true, I found that the reasons for women to join the LTTE were more varied. I actually asked a few dozen female members of varying age and length of time with the LTTE for their reasons for joining. It was an interesting mix that fell into eight broad categories.

To punish the Lankan Military for killing someone they loved: Girls joined because a close family member had been affected. Prior to 2002, an unknown number of civilians, well in excess of 40,000, had been killed by the Lankan Military and Sinhala thugs during the five decades of conflict. There was no shortage of girls whose family members had been directly affected by the killings and disappearances. Girls cited this as the most common reason for joining. They all expressed an urge to punish the military for what it had done to their families.

To avoid falling victim to sexual violence by the enemy military: During the 80s and 90s rape by the military, both Lankan and Indian, was very prevalent. Also, with numerous military camps set near schools, school girls faced regular sexual harassment by the military. Often the military would insist on body checking the girls before letting them inside. Many girls reported male military members suspiciously touching their sanitary pads during the body checks. Girls joined LTTE, outraged by this violence against other girls. Joining the movement made them feel empowered rather than a potential victim. At the risk of stating the obvious, it must be said that the pull to join LTTE was especially strong because girls felt secure in the LTTE movement, within which sexual harassment and rape was totally absent.

Displacement and lack of regular schooling: As the war progressed over a period of two decades people displaced multiple times losing their homes and possessions each time they displaced. Sometimes these displacements would be anticipated and organized. Often during military attacks people displaced many times in chaotic conditions often living under trees while on the move. They would eventually end up in crowded camps for the displaced, mostly in public buildings like schools. They would continue to live in these crowded camps for several months until they could set up a rudimentary home somewhere in the displaced location. Such conditions took away the normal life for the young girls. Continuous bombing and shelling also disrupted the schools. These factors created a fertile environment for a young girl to join the LTTE. Joining the movement gave purpose and order to their life.

Senior female LTTE members as role models: In Tamil society, young girls did not move freely and independently in the community. Their dress code was also fairly strict. Most girls would not be allowed to wear trousers. Seeing female LTTE members, self-confident and well-dressed in smart trousers, brought out a desire in civilian girls to be like them. LTTE members in general moved freely within the community. They visited them, had meals with them, and helped them. This brought the female members into close contact with the civilian girls, creating in them a desire to follow suit.

Extreme poverty (domestic duty, no school): As a result of: death of bread winners in the family, multiple displacements, and the economic blockade by the Lankan government, families reached extreme levels of poverty. In the families most affected by poverty, the girl child's education was the first casualty. She was often expected to stay home and take on the duties of the mother and let the mother go out to earn money as a daily wage laborer. Girls rebelled against this and joined the LTTE.

LTTE awareness campaign: The LTTE conducted extensive political education campaigns in the community, and this had an effect on both the boys and the girls, moving them to join the movement.

Rebellion against the traditional culture: Tamil society, like many traditional societies, had arranged marriages, and girls, even if they desired to, could not escape it. Dowry was also a humiliating practice for many girls. If not for the LTTE, these girls would have had no plausible channel to rebel against the restrictive traditions of their society. Joining the LTTE provided that channel. The LTTE was an attractive option for these girls because of the LTTE policies promoting women's rights and banishing dowries.

Abuse of one form or other in the family: There were several cases of girls joining the LTTE to escape sexual abuse at home. In Tamil society, and indeed in the entire of South Asia, sensitive handling of this issue had not been developed nationally. It remained unspoken. By joining the LTTE, these victims were able to escape the abuse without having to face exposing the culprit.

Female membership structure

The involvement of women in the armed struggle was present from the beginning, when they served mainly as carers, providing meals, and caring for the wounded. Then the concept of *Suthanthira Paravaikal* (freedom birds) was introduced in the 1980s. A women's organization and publication carrying this name were launched. Once women started to join the LTTE as arms-carrying members, this organization died a natural death. But the women's section of the LTTE political division continued the publication of *Suthanthira Paravaikal* until the end, but with much reduced vigor.

Between male and female members a degree of separation was maintained within the LTTE. They did come together for executing specific tasks, both in civilian and military spheres. Two opposing views on whether this separation assisted or hindered women's development prevailed in Vanni. On the one hand was the view that it permitted freer development of women, which was similar to the theory that girls-only schools are good for girls. The implementation of discipline was also seen as better when it was carried out in segregated spaces. On the other hand was the view that women lost out on exposure to male-dominated knowledge and skills because of too much separation. I believe that in Vanni the tension between these two views was being gradually resolved as men and women came together more and more to do tasks in many spheres.

The majority of the female members within LTTE reported directly to female leaders. This hierarchy was intercepted somewhere up the chain by a male leader. In the case of military divisions, this interception by a male leader would only be at the very top, Pirapaaharan himself. Within the political division of LTTE, there was a separate women's section with a female leader. All female members within the political division of the LTTE eventually reported to this female leader up the hierarchy. She in turn reported to the leader of the political division, invariably a male, who in turn reported to the LTTE leader, Pirapaaharan.

However, there existed another parallel group of about twenty female leaders from all divisions. This group met Pirapaaharan regularly to discuss issues relating to women. Many male leaders viewed this special access that women leaders had as a privilege. Many senior male leaders of similar ranking did not have this kind of access. Pulitheevan often expressed frustration that the women leaders failed to exploit the special privilege they had in order to further women's rights within the movement. I, too, had requested, through women leaders in the political division who were part of the group that regularly met Pirapaaharan,[15] that some issues related to women be raised and resolved. I observed some reluctance on the part of these women leaders to be assertive.

In many institutions, female LTTE members often had to work under the leadership of a male LTTE leader; this occurred more frequently in non-military divisions like the political division. These female members working under male leaders ended up having two leaders to whom they had to report. An unwritten understanding was that in all work-related matters they took orders from their male leader, whereas all other matters, such as discipline etc., were dealt with by their female leader. This issue of two leaderships remained contentious and was not fully resolved. It must also be mentioned that LTTE male members also sometimes reported to female leaders, and this was seen as very normal.

Reasons for the loss of vigor

There had been ongoing work on women's issues within the LTTE for decades. Ideas on women's issues within the LTTE evolved during a time when the LTTE controlled Jaffna from the late 1980s to the early 1990s. The massive drive against the system of dowry-giving by the bride's family was carried out by the LTTE, with full participation by female members. Adele Balasingkam's book, *Unbroken Chain,* on the historical evolution of the dowry system, was also published by the LTTE at this time. With the mass exodus from Jaffna to Vanni in 1995, the LTTE center also shifted from Jaffna to Vanni. This shift from Jaffna, where there was access to a richer intellectual life, to Vanni resulted in a lessened focus on women's issues.

During my stay in Vanni, I was able to observe another important factor that had over the years led to a decline in the sum of the intellectual caliber of the members. In the modern business model, skilled people are a most valuable asset. In LTTE, not only was this model ignored, but for the sake of egalitarianism, everyone was expected to serve in frontline duties. This had resulted in the decimation of some of the best minds within the LTTE at a very young age. I was able to observe this very clearly among the women. Some of the women who would have evolved into strong leaders advocating for women's rights had been killed in battles. Head hunters in the business world know that it is not easy to replace such people with special knowledge and skills. Barathy and Vanathy were two well-known female members with leadership qualities, who were killed in the 1990s. One did not come across many members with such qualities in Vanni during this period.

In a microcosm

There was an ongoing debate in Vanni on the female civilian attire. On several occasions, I had been part of this debate. Trivial as it may have been, this debate represented in a microcosm the forces acting for and against a more liberated female culture in Vanni.

A visually exhilarating sign of women's liberation in Vanni was the sight of confident-looking LTTE women in their non-military LTTE attire of black pants, light colored loosely fitting shirt with a belt worn over it. A similarly smart uniform was also worn by LTTE police women. Many outside observers had been impressed by the sight of these women in smart-looking and relatively liberating attire in this part of the world. Yet, visually, the most obvious sign of oppressive habits among civilian women in Vanni was also the practice of wearing the *saree* by even those employed in LTTE civilian institutions. Thousands of civilian women worked in such institutions, and they were all compelled to wear the *saree* in a uniform style determined by that LTTE institution. The contrast was striking for anyone who cared to observe it. It was shocking to see the *saree* being made compulsory for civilian women working in LTTE institutions, when LTTE women wore trousers and shirts as their uniform. Many young women have told me that they resisted applying for jobs in LTTE institutions because of the compulsion to wear the *saree*. Almost all women resisted this practice. LTTE women were vocal about their resistance and they were never subjected to it. Civilian women on the other hand were subjected to this rule. The *saree* rule was invariably made and enforced by senior male LTTE leaders within various LTTE institutions.

There was another important aspect to this microcosmic view of using the uniform rule for civilian women to depict the status of female liberation under the LTTE. There is one story that senior female LTTE members repeated about how women first joined the movement as arms-carrying members. The story goes like this. It was vehemently resisted by almost all the senior LTTE male members. LTTE leader Pirapaaharan nevertheless implemented this, dismissing all objections. The typical and now well-known female non-military LTTE attire of trouser and shirt was also vehemently resisted by the senior male LTTE members who said it would not be accepted by the community at large. Pirapaaharan dismissed this objection too, and he was proved right.

These different tensions acting on the issue of female attire accurately captured the status of women's issues in general in Vanni. LTTE women and a large section of the civilian women had a heightened awareness; the LTTE leader, Pirapaaharan, appeared to have understood some of the basic issues, but the other senior LTTE male leaders were lagging behind. Pirapaaharan was reputed to have said that his senior male leaders carried out all the tasks he assigned to them well beyond his expectations, but when it came to issues of women's rights, they were failing abysmally. This was not to say that there were no other senior male LTTE members who understood the women's rights issues. Indeed, I, too, came to know of some who did.

Ongoing efforts

In 2008, when Ilanko took over the police department from Nadeesan after the demise of Thamilselvan, to my astonishment he initiated many pro-women programs within the police force. He organized training for all the female police officers to deal with women-related issues. Bearing in mind that the majority of the female police officers were young women with only limited training in the police force, this targeted training of women related-issues was a new area of knowledge for these young women. Unfortunately, the program never had a chance to prove its worth due to the multiple displacements starting from 2008 till the end war. I had the opportunity to have close interactions with Ilanko in regard to this project to train female police officers. His understanding of the issues and his one hundred percent pro-woman stance was so refreshing and heartwarming. He told me that he had produced awareness-raising dramas in the past on women's issues. He expressed frustration that the LTTE women in Vanni were not more pro-active in this area. Ilanko's fate after the war remains unknown. It is suspected that he was also among the hundreds who were either killed or made to disappear following capture by the Lankan Military as they walked out of the war zone during the end the war in 2009.

During this period, a wide-ranging program was instituted to encourage the learning of karate among both boys and girls. Vanni-wide competitions were also conducted for all age groups. Learning karate by girls of all ages was a revolutionary idea among Tamils, and it contributed to the development and advancement of women in many ways. Indeed, an LTTE woman who had gone through military training could be readily picked out even if she was wearing traditional female attire. She usually had a slightly broader shoulder, a smart walking style, and the habit of looking straight ahead rather than looking down to the ground. I believe these traits were slowly catching up with the general female population, and the karate training was assisting in this process.

Married LTTE couples

The vast majority of married LTTE couples also appeared to have much healthier relationships than what I had observed in the Tamil community in general. I attribute many factors to this healthy state of affairs. These couples, as part of their work, had extensive involvement in the public sphere outside the home through which they drew much satisfaction. This reduced the chance of dissatisfaction in the relationship. The respect LTTE men give to women was well above what could be observed among civilians. This, too, derived from the respect they had for the work LTTE women did. The other side of this behavior was that LTTE women were articulate and assertive without fear of violence from their partner, which contributed to their sense of well being.

Also, given the large number of young widows, remarriage was a lot more common than on the rest of the island. This was true for both civilians and LTTE members. It was very refreshing. Some LTTE members had sought to marry wives of *maaveerar* and I knew many such happily married couples.

My role

As my perspective of women's issues evolved over a period of three years during my time there, I saw a contrast between the plight of many women and a latent potential that did not exist outside Vanni. I was eager to work to unleash this latent potential. In 2008, I had more time because the role of the Peace Secretariat was diminishing and my involvement in NESoHR was limited to writing reports. Without realizing the fact that the extra time had become available to me due to the evolving crisis, I embarked on my long-cherished aim of involving myself in women's issues. After some dithering, it became clear to me that domestic violence could be the subject that would serve the purpose well. At CWDR we gathered some LTTE and some civilian women to discuss the means by which this could be taken further. The latent potential was very evident at these meetings. I was particularly impressed by one married civilian woman who demonstrated an understanding of the woman's issues and showed leadership potential. I saw it as a sign of the diffusion of the pro-woman character of the LTTE into the wider society.

In my eagerness for thoroughness, I proposed an in-depth survey on domestic violence in Vanni society. I drew up the survey questions and CWDR organized a week-long training session for a selection of thirty women to carry out the survey. This survey ended up as a big failure because of inadequacy in human resources and planning. I am not sure whom to blame for this failure, but I was truly disappointed. The CWDR head, Kalaimahal, then came to the rescue and promised to provide me with collated statistics of the women whom CWDR had helped over the years. Her office did an excellent job of collating these statistics.

Kalaimahal headed the CWDR. She had not had much schooling. Her family lived in Jaffna. After her mother died when she was nine years old, her father remarried. Kalaimahal and her siblings were sent to the Karunaa Illam, a children's home in Kilinochchi run by a church. From here, her sister ran away to join the LTTE. In order to get her sister released, Kalaimahal ran away too and joined the LTTE. During the 1990s she was taking part in battles in Batticaloa. Here, she was once given up as dead and her body was stacked with other bodies of dead cadres. She was rescued after someone noticed her moving. During the *Jeyasikkuru* battles in Vanni in late 1990s, she was injured in her stomach and lost the ability to have babies.

At one stage, Kalaimahal was the political coordinator for an area in Vanni, a role mostly given to male members. This was an indication of her administrative skill. She was made the head of the CWDR prior to the 2002 ceasefire. Her administrative skills and her drive were phenomenal. She built up the CWDR to amazing heights. She fell in love with a fellow LTTE member whom she married, and they adopted an abandoned newborn girl. I last met Kalaimahal in March 2009, still with the same drive, living among destitute women and children who were under the care of CWDR. She introduced me to four siblings whom they had just taken in because their parents were killed in artillery fire only a few days earlier.

I have spoken to other CWDR employees and beneficiaries who walked out of the war zone with Kalaimahal and her assistant, Gowri, and their families during the end war in 2009. Kalaimahal, her husband, their three-year-old daughter, and Gowri and her husband were taken away by the Lankan Military. They are among the hundreds who disappeared following capture by the Lankan Military after the end war in 2009.

While living at the CWDR hostel, I came to know many women, both LTTE members and civilians. One of them was Varatha, an LTTE member. She belonged to the military division but visited Kalaimahal, her cousin, often. I can still picture the total abandonment with which Varatha played with Kalaimahal's three-year-old daughter and their loud laughter together. Varatha had the capacity to play like a three-year-old and there was absolutely no pretense in her play. Varatha was from the Sothiya regiment, one of the two LTTE female military regiments. The other one was the Malathy regiment. Both were named after female *maaveerar*. One common game that Varatha and the three-year-old played was to ask the child what regiment she belonged to. The child's response would swing between one of the two female regiments, often throwing Varatha into loud howls of despair when the child says she belonged to the other regiment. In late 2008, Varatha sustained a head injury during a battle. Kalaimahal cared for her in the hospital. I last saw Varatha in 2009 walking on Maaththalan road. She was killed during the final phase of war.

Kalaimahal gave me the collated statistics on domestic violence. I compared this with other published statistics that were available on the internet and found that the pattern was similar. In other words, domestic violence occurred with the same frequency in Vanni as it did in Lanka and parts of India, and even compared similarly with what was published in pamphlets on domestic violence in the UK—that 30 percent of the women who received CWDR assistance reported domestic violence by their partner. In Vanni there was a widely held view that alcohol was a primary factor in domestic violence, though this was challenged by the available literature. CWDR statistics also showed that only 60 percent of the women reported the assailant was under the influence of alcohol. I wrote a paper in Tamil summarizing what I had learnt and gave it to Kalaimahal for decision on further action. In our next group meeting, we decided that in the weekly issue of the *Vellinatham* paper we would publish a true story on domestic violence that the group members had directly dealt with.

People gave me handwritten stories, and I typed and collated more than twenty such stories. None of us expected the editor of the paper, a male, to resist publishing the stories weekly. Two senior female LTTE leaders attempted to persuade the editor, without much success. This was despite the fact that *Vellinatham* had a section devoted to women. We were all flabbergasted. The editor apparently thought the time was not right for such material, while an intensive war was going on. The group then decided to do a billboard campaign. A lot of effort was spent on creating scenes of domestic violence that were photographed. Captions were added to these photographs. An international agency, OXFAM, that was active in Vanni, agreed to fund this campaign. The designs were handed to it for making the billboards. Discussions were underway for permission to erect the billboards. Around this time we displaced from Kilinochchi. My efforts and dreams of working on women's issues in Vanni came to an end.

12

Vanni
social space

My narrative of my positive and personal experience of Vanni comes to end with the last chapter. I still would like to give the reader an overview of Vanni which I have not included in my own narrative so far. This chapter and the next, then, give a big picture view of Vanni, only a small part of which I experienced.

The Vanni population during my stay there was an interesting mixture of Tamils. There was a minority population of Tamils who had lived there for generations. Another minority, which had lived in Vanni for two to three generations, had moved there when the state allocated forest land to people who cleared it and made it into farmland. Another minority of upcountry Tamil people had moved there due to poverty and violence against them. The 1995 exodus from Jaffna to Vanni resulted in another large section of the Vanni population. Similar, but smaller-scale, migrations had also taken place from other parts of Tamil Eelam whenever Tamils faced violence in their hometown. It was a mix of people who had suffered most at the hands of the Lankan Military, but who could not afford to escape the island. They found sanctuary in the LTTE part of Tamil Eelam. This mixed population, who had been sensitized to the oppression by the Lankan state, presented an ideal demography for social engineering. The pervasive presence of the LTTE within this population did manage to create a community that had adopted the attitude of struggle and displayed some very unique features.

Past traumas pervaded the life of the people of Vanni. One could sit down and chat to literally anyone living in Vanni and hear their personal stories of war-related tragedies. Even prior to 2002, literally everyone in Vanni held such traumatic memories in their hearts. It was this group of people who also nourished hope and built up Vanni into a thriving area during the ceasefire. Many expatriate staff of international agencies, who came to Vanni in large numbers following the 2004 December tsunami, had been impressed by this society's grit in the face of repeated traumas. Besides LTTE, there was another important contributing factor—Tamil culture. It had many facets that gave the society the stamina to withstand trauma. This culture is concerned about other people's affairs and leaves no one isolated. It is the duty of everyone to intimately share other people's tragedies and joy. This culture effectively uses food sharing, especially during times of tragedy or joy, for social cohesion. The people's open abandonment in crying out loudly to express trauma also creates cohesion among the people. The children, as the common property of the community, also give an additional cohesion. In essence, these pre-existing cultural traits helped to increase social cohesion in the face of trauma. It is this cohesion that gave them the mental stamina to withstand trauma and hold up hope.

Civilian religions

The ordinary folks in Vanni, who were mostly Hindus and Catholics, like ordinary folks everywhere, were very religious. They were more religious than the people in Jaffna, who exhibited a greater degree of Westernization. Temple festivals were occasions where this was clearly visible. All types of *kaavadi,* which involves a ritual of self mutilation, were practiced widely during the temple festivals. It is said that these rituals were revived and practiced more widely to cope with war-related traumas. Indeed some of these practices had also been revived in Jaffna where it had almost completely died down three decades earlier. *Gowri Viratham,* six days of fasting except for milk and fruit at night, was observed by women of all walks of life. Those who took part wore a string tied to their upper arm, which was publicly visible. I think this was displayed with pride, and its cultural meaning crossed religious boundaries and was tinted with the prevailing attitude of struggle.

There are many aspects of the Tamil struggle that are worth a more detailed study, and one of these is the role played by the Catholic clergy and the Catholic people. Though there were many fractures and estrangements as the struggle progressed, the early support of the Catholic Church was unmistakable. It had parallels to the role of Catholic clergy in Central American struggles like that of Guatemala, which was rooted in latter day ideas of liberation theology. It was also true that a lot of the fisher folks in the homeland were Catholics, and due to the dominance of sea faring within the LTTE, this special nexus also could have strengthened it. There was a particular church-temple in Mullaithiivu, *Kulanthai Jesu* temple, which translated is "Baby Jesus" temple. Its appearance and practices crossed Hindu-Catholic practices, and it was very popular among all the people. The blurring of the two religious practices, Hindu and Catholic, was interesting and was clearly a side effect of LTTE membership and constituency, brought together by the attitude of struggle.

The *Vattaapali Kannaki Amman* temple in Mullaithiivu and its annual *ponkal* event, falling sometime during the month of May, had a special place in the Vanni calendar. This event used to draw huge crowds from all over the homeland. The traditions of this temple were unique to the area and rooted in the very ancient local culture of *Kannaki* worship. Even after the area became isolated as war intensified, this remained an important event in the Vanni calendar and the only official religious holiday that was observed specifically in this area.

The LTTE had no religion

LTTE was a secular organization. Thus, in contrast to the civilian community, the LTTE community displayed secular characteristics. The social life of married and unmarried LTTE members was different. Unmarried LTTE members lived a distinctly separate life in smaller units with an appointed leader. The size of these units varied widely. Their needs were all met by the organization and their time was entirely dedicated to the tasks assigned to them by the organization. Thus their social life was about work and enjoying the company of fellow members. Indeed, they did not have the space to practice religion even if they had wanted to, though they could retain their faith.

After a specified number of years of service in the organization, LTTE members were permitted to marry. They had the freedom to choose their partner, but the space for courting was non-existent—though talking in public was permitted. Once they had chosen a partner, they could seek permission from the organization to marry, even prior to reaching the required number of years of service. Once such permission was granted their pairing became public knowledge and as the LTTE expected such a commitment to be permanent it was not easy to break this without due process. Once married, LTTE families lived among the wider community, and often members of their extended families would also live with them. These LTTE families were also distinctly non-religious in their family life, though some would have retained their original family faith.

Remembering the maaveerar

Memories of LTTE members killed in battles had a pervasive presence in the life of LTTE members. A special word was used to refer to their death, *veeramaranam* (heroic death), and the deceased LTTE members were referred to as *maaveerar*, meaning "great hero". Their death would never be referred to as death but always as *veeramaranam* or *veerachcha* in colloquial speech. The place where they were buried was referred to as the *maaveerar-thuyilum-illam* or *thuyilum-illam* for short, meaning "great heroes' resting place". The killed or dead LTTE members were buried, in contrast to the prevailing majority tradition of cremation. This burial was referred to as *vithaiththal,* which in Tamil means "planting of a seed". The symbolism was that a member was not dead and gone, but had gone down as a seed for new ones to come up. The Tamil word used to refer to living LTTE members was *poorali,* meaning "the one who fights for justice". These five words, *poorali, veeramaranam, maaveerar, vithaiththal,* and *thuyilum-illam,* were in common usage and created a special cultural context in the life of the people and the members alike. Pictures of *maaveerar* hung in most homes, both LTTE and civilian.

The *thuyilum-illam(s)* were very imposing sites and as an iconography it never failed to elicit strong feelings among the people in Vanni. People paid respect as they went past these sites in a manner similar to what they would do as they went past a temple or a church. For mothers and fathers whose son or daughter may have been resting in it, it had a powerful pull. I knew young LTTE mothers who took their young children to play among the gravestones and described the experience as peaceful and calming—one that was akin to going to temple. People had a genuine feeling of respect and gratitude for the *maaveerar.*

Another feature notable among the LTTE community was the level of devotion they exhibited to long-serving members. Besides Pirapaaharan, such devotion also was directed towards many other most-senior members. Sometime in 2006, late Brigadier Balraj once visited the Peace Secretariat. It was the only time I saw him. I was fascinated and impressed by the awe and respect that LTTE members at the Peace Secretariat awarded him. I came to sense this devotion more forcefully when such leaders either died or were killed. In this regard, the deaths of Balraj and Thamilselvan during this period stand out in my memory.

LTTE divisions in civilian space

Sometime during 2006, there was an effort inside the LTTE Peace Secretariat to lay out LTTE institutions as they fitted within the wider LTTE structure, for publication on its website. The effort, however, was prevented for reasons of security.

Based on this effort and my own observations, a very rough LTTE structure is shown in this figure above. There were multitudes of substructures within each of these wings, with the political wing having the most subdivisions visible to civilians. Notable sub-institutions under the political wing included, in order of size, all the welfare institutions for destitute children, women, and the old; media services; the courts; some healthcare services; an economic division that assisted farmers as well as others doing some other economic activities; a sports division; an education division; and a cultural division. The police force came under a separate wing of its own. My own experiences, which form the basis of this book, were mainly within the political wing's sphere of influence.

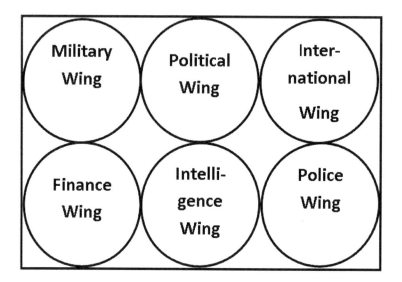

The finance wing was the next most visible division. It operated many food and grocery outlets, as well as some manufacturing outfits. This division, through its retailing, manufacturing, farming, transport, and banking activities, employed a large number of civilians. The goal of this division was to provide services to LTTE and civilians alike, and to raise the funds needed to run the huge machinery that was the LTTE-run de-facto state. I have no idea about the monetary size of these ventures.

The international wing also had a presence in Vanni, but it mattered very little to the local population unless they had friends or relatives from the Diaspora visiting them. These Diaspora visitors, however, could not escape contact with the international wing. They would be interviewed and issued an exit pass to leave Vanni. In the current post-LTTE-defeat phase, ex-LTTE members who had escaped to the affluent Western countries have struggled to portray a continued existence of the LTTE, which at best is tenuous on several fronts. I personally find such an existence of the LTTE in affluent countries to be without the essence that Vanni once exhibited.

While the political, finance, and international divisions had the appearance of civil organizations operating in the public space, the same cannot be said about the military and intelligence divisions, which had very little public presence. Interestingly, it was a UNICEF staff member who once told me that next door to their office was one of the intelligence division's "bases", which was the term used to refer to residence cum sub-offices of the various LTTE sections. Thus, while the intelligence division bases were scattered throughout the public space, their presence was not felt. As far as I know, the military wing did not even have bases with whom public interaction was possible. It appeared to me that the LTTE military space was far removed from the public space. While this separation may not have been always the case, in Vanni at that time the military division did appear to be very security conscious.

Underscoring LTTE philosophy that there could be no self-governance without the military strength to protect it, all LTTE members were trained for military action, and most were later called upon for frontline duty. LTTE members shared a sense of togetherness that did not recognize the internal structural divisions of the LTTE. Members of similar ranks socialized more freely, and even seniors, except for the few top most leaders, often joined in. Social interaction between male and female members was not as free, though it existed. I was lucky enough to gain the confidence of members to the extent that my presence in the vicinity did not alter the group social behavior. However, if I made any attempts to directly enter the group interaction, it always altered the dynamics.

Naturally one heard more about the military side as war intensified inside Vanni. Loss of life on the front lines became frequent, and the recruitment drive picked up in intensity. As batches of new recruits graduated, parents were invited for the graduation ceremony. LTTE members from the political division also frequently attended these functions when someone close to them was graduating. Though I, too, was asked to go with them, I never felt inclined, and I never went to any such function, which I now regret. I was also once offered a visit to military training places, but I never demonstrated any interest and never saw any such installations. Due to my disinterest in the military side, I also did not have the opportunity to meet many Black Tigers.[16]

LTTE-civilian interconnectedness

The interface between LTTE and civilians at large had many facets, and the result was a highly integrated social space, where the distinction between the two gradually blurred. The emotional connection civilians had towards LTTE as the liberation fighters was always there. On top of this basic emotional connection, other layers of interconnectedness were created over a period spanning many decades. Though only a very small percentage of those living in Vanni at this time were bona fide LTTE members, a rough estimate of the total number of LTTE members at this period, present, past and killed would be 50,000. Thus the majority of working age people in Vanni had a close relative from this pool. This factor strongly colored the social space in Vanni at this time and gave the entire society an LTTE flavor. LTTE institutions were also the major employer, and as a result civilians were further drawn into the LTTE ambit. The large number of LTTE families with children now living in the wider community also brought in another layer of interconnectedness.

This growing interconnectedness was constantly negated by some of the activities of the LTTE. Foremost among these activities was the ever-present recruitment drive of the LTTE. During this period, the bureaucratic lethargy in some LTTE institutions also came under constant criticism. This was mainly due to the shortage in human resource capacity, which failed to match the growing role being played by the LTTE. I repeatedly heard people saying that the LTTE was increasing its distance from the people.

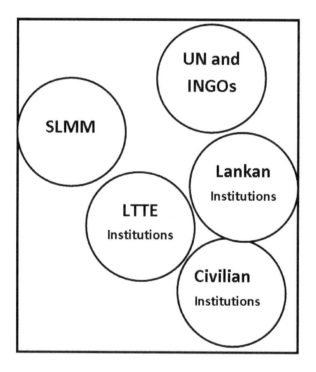

There was a cultural gap between LTTE families living in the wider community and the civilian community. The rest of the community kept a respectful distance from LTTE families, even if they were neighbors. The reasons for this distancing were due to the non-religious, egalitarian social practices of the LTTE families. The women of LTTE families in particular had developed patterns of behavior of assertiveness that would not sit well in the base society. The blurring of this distinction was gradual. Other families with immediate LTTE connections inter-acted more freely with LTTE families, and families of steady supporters also had stronger relationships with LTTE families.

Outside agencies

The ceasefire, the peace process, as well as the 2004 tsunami that badly destroyed many parts of the island, including parts of Vanni, had created a large presence of international agencies: SLMM, UN agencies and international NGOs. This also provided employment as well as an injection of money into the area.

Lankan controlled local government institutions also functioned in Vanni. This feature in Vanni would not be common in other parts of the world controlled by non-state actors. This feature had persisted in the island for nearly two decades. These bodies practically had no autonomy. They employed Tamils to administer but took their policy direction and orders from the Lankan central government. The majority of the Tamil employees of these Lankan local government bodies also identified with the struggle of the LTTE.

The salaries and wages of those employed by the international agencies were at least twice as high as those working in the Lankan institutions, which in turn were higher than that of the civilians working in LTTE institutions. The greatest number of people in Vanni, however, were involved in private farming and fishing activities.

LTTE had well-established institutions that mirrored and linked with the Lankan controlled local government institutions functioning in Vanni. The mode of these linkages varied depending on the institutions, but every Lankan institution worked in tandem with the corresponding mirrored LTTE institution. The most closely interlinked was probably the health sector. There were several reasons for this close cooperation. The Lankan health sector in Vanni was poorly staffed, whereas there were trained and experienced health workers in the corresponding LTTE health institution, and these workers filled some of the gaps in the Lankan health institution. LTTE members had attended mainstream universities and graduated as medical doctors. I saw the medical workers in the Lankan institutions as well as the LTTE health institutions reporting to health-related meetings called by Thamilselvan. Also, because health sector institutions were frequented by people from all walks of life, the line of separation between the Lankan health sector and the LTTE health sector was very much blurred.

The LTTE education sector on the other hand was not well developed, and the LTTE from the beginning made no attempt to develop its own educational institution for the children. The mirror institution, however, did two things worth noting. It maintained a cordial working relationship with the Lankan education institution, i.e. the school system, and it made efforts to correct the grave errors that were being made in teaching children their own history. I personally doubt that it was very successful in this second effort. The mirror institution conducted other services independent of the Lankan education service, such as helping poor students with financial tutoring assistance. The mirror institution also was the point of contact for involving schools in civilian-based LTTE led activities, such as marking important days, protest marches etc. Mirror LTTE institutions also maintained links with the Lankan-controlled Tamil managed agriculture department, road development authority and also the District Secretariats.

The leaders of each of these mirror LTTE institutions and the top executives of the corresponding Lankan institutions would have had close working relationships. Sometimes the executives of the Lankan institutions would have to take orders from their LTTE counterparts. For the most part, the executives of the Lankan institutions managed the demands of two warring parties well. The majority of employees in the Lankan institutions functioning in Vanni, who were all Tamils, took orders only from their Lankan executive. They could thus remain more or less aloof to the twin authority under which they were working.

International agencies also had this same balancing act to play, but their own mandates often protected them from undue interference from the twin authorities in Vanni. These agencies were treated cordially by the LTTE, but there was always a lurking suspicion of their motives. The three-pronged drive against LTTE child-soldier recruitment by UNICEF, SLMM, and ICRC was a constant irritant. Also causing concern were any efforts by any of the international agencies to collect statistics on Vanni people. I can only guess that the fear was that these statistics might be used against the LTTE for propaganda purposes. The communication between international agencies and the LTTE was also limited by cultural and language issues. As far as I know, except in the case of the LTTE Peace Secretariat and the head of LTTE political division, all communications involving the LTTE and International agencies were facilitated by interpreters employed by the international agencies, and thus had an inherent bias towards their views and against the LTTE. In my view, a better communication channel that represented the LTTE side more favorably was painfully absent.

Some of the institutions under the political wing of the LTTE sought and obtained funds from Lankan and international agencies for specific projects to serve civilians. Such institutions would be staffed mostly by civilians, but having an LTTE member as the decision making executive. There would also be a few more members within these institutions in decision-making positions. For the most part, these institutions functioned like a civilian institution except for this fact. Anyone who worked in these institutions would have been aware of its connection to the LTTE through its executive. For the beneficiaries and others, this was neither obvious nor relevant. I worked closely with two such institutions, the Centre for Women's Development and Rehabilitation (CWDR) and the Centre for Health Care (CHC). It was obvious that the control of these organizations by LTTE members made them free of corruption and gave the entire institution a culture of genuine service mentality. Due to the international and Lankan media onslaught on LTTE in general, and the Tamil Rehabilitation Organization (TRO) in particular, openly saying institutions were under the control of the LTTE evoked negative views and emotions.

The TRO is the largest local NGO that was functioning in Vanni. The TRO was implementing wide-ranging programs in Vanni that included caring for destitute children, micro-assistance to the self employed, and village development programs. It also operated a demining branch called the Humanitarian Demining Unit (HDU) together with a Norwegian NGO. The TRO also had an extensive funding collection activity among the Tamil Diaspora for funding these programs. Many international NGOs operating in Vanni partnered with the TRO for many of the programs they were implementing. After the 2002 ceasefire, the TRO also operated an office from Colombo. However, in 2007, the TRO was accused of funding LTTE terrorism by the international community. The accusation was led by Canada, and TRO became a banned organization in many Western countries.

I have no firsthand knowledge of TRO funding issues. I was confident that the funds obtained by CWDR and CHC were not diverted for any other purposes by their respective executives. Indeed, I have had in-depth discussions with the executive of CWDR on many occasions about funds they obtained. I always tried to read between the lines to detect any signs of misappropriation of the funds, and I detected none. Though LTTE institutions in general were always keen to advertise the services it provided to civilians, the civilian facade of some of its institutions was clearly aimed at making it acceptable to Lankan and international agencies in order that they might fund them—or at least not impede their funding drives.

13

Consolidation during the ceasefire

The signing of the 2002 ceasefire agreement spurred a hive of development activities in Vanni. This region had been subjected to extreme restrictions on the flow of people and goods since the mass exodus of people from Jaffna in October 1995. The majority of the people who left Jaffna had moved into the Vanni region. The 2002 ceasefire opened up the A9 route that ran through Vanni all the way to Jaffna. People, mainly Tamils, and goods traffic flooded the A9 route. The opening of the A9 route, international aid, and Diaspora funding spurred a lot of development activities in Vanni. This was the scene that welcomed the visitors who cared to visit Vanni at this time. During the early part of my time in Vanni, the mood among the people was positive and the visible face of Vanni was changing through development in every possible facet of life.

Education: During the earlier war-phase, a large number of school-aged children had dropped out of school. A massive drive was undertaken to ensure every child attended school. Several educational institutions for school leavers came into being, and foremost among them were the IT education services. Vanni-Tech and several other IT training institutions that worked closely with Vanni-Tech came into existence and were funded by the Diaspora. Buildings for several other educational institutions were underway in a specially allocated area in Kilinochchi named *Ariviyal nakaram,* which translates to "knowledge town". Many types of learning institutions were planned or underway for this knowledge town. These included institutions for training medical professionals, language learning centers—specifically Tamil and English—and special education schools for the war-affected youth and the less able youth.

Health: The Thileepan primary care medical service of LTTE had been in existence for more than a decade and catered to remote areas where people did not have access to any other medical service. After the ceasefire this was supplemented with other health care institutions. The Centre for

Health Care aimed to undertake broader medical services, including the education of primary health care professionals. The private Ponnambalam hospital, which had branches in Kilinochchi and Mullaithiivu, expanded its facilities and services during this period. Several of the destroyed hospitals were rebuilt during this period. Medical experts from the Diaspora visited and provided free specialist treatment, including plastic surgery, for those injured in the war.

Disability service: One of the outstanding features of Vanni society was the degree of integration of disabled people into the mainstream. They could be seen actively participating in many spheres, carrying out work with grit and amazing agility. People with one arm would ride motorbikes with heavy loads behind them on their motorbikes. You would hardly have known that some people you worked with were missing a leg from below the knee. Disability had been normalized. Serving these people was the only prosthetic-fitting service in Vanni, Venpuraa. This also expanded its service with the introduction of new technology. A common phrase one heard even prior to the Mullivaikaal genocide was about so and so having a piece of shrapnel in some part of their body. Many people lived with such pieces in their body and suffered varying degrees of pain as a result. Visiting medical experts did their best to remove the ones causing the most severe pain.

Welfare: The TRO, which was responsible for running innumerable welfare institutions, ranging from children's homes to village development programs, grew in size. The CWDR, which supplemented some of the services provided by the TRO, specifically targeting women, also expanded in size and added new buildings. The CWDR was run entirely by women and thus had a distinct character of its own. In addition to the numerous children's homes that cared for parentless and also very poor children, there were many other types of welfare institutions catering to civilians, as well as disabled LTTE members. Anpuchchoolai, for old people, especially destitute parents of *maaveerar,* was started in this period. There was Mayoori-illam for battle-scarred wheelchair-bound female LTTE members. Navamarivukkoodam was an educational institute that retrained injured LTTE members in skills suitable to their physical disability. All of these welfare institutions were upgraded with better facilities.

Courts: Even prior to 2002, the LTTE had its own set of laws, a college to train its lawyers, and an extensive courts system supported in turn by a police division and prisons. These institutions employed large numbers of civilians to work in the courts system and the police force.

The division within this system which wrote the laws, independent of the Lanka law, for the emerging state of Tamil Eelam, was also active during the ceasefire period, producing new laws on two high profile issues: land ownership and the age of recruitment into military service.

Childcare: Thalir, a chain of day care centers for children of LTTE families, was another notable institution that grew in size and quality during this period. The service, provided free of charge, was perhaps the best such facility on the entire island. The staff to child ratio was very high. Though the majority of the carers were not well trained, they were under the strict supervision of some mature, dedicated female members, who ensured that high standards were maintained. All LTTE mothers were expected to report to work one year after childbirth and this service was aimed at these mothers.

Human rights & environment: The human rights body NESoHR and the Environment Management Centre were launched.

Children's park: A children's park cum zoo was built in Kilinochchi and named Chanthiran poonga. It was a great hit with children as well as adults. People from all around Vanni visited the zoo. The roadside just outside of the park would be filled with pavement sellers of all types of wares. The mini zoo had scores of local birds as well as many local mammals. It also had crocodiles, which were a major attraction. The area thus displayed a festive atmosphere during school holidays.

Bookshops & libraries: A bookshop chain called Arivamuthu sold books needed by school children, as well as an excellent selection of books in Tamil covering a wide range of topics. I gained a great deal of knowledge reading books from this bookshop. The many tiny libraries scattered across Vanni had a near-complete collection of LTTE literature that had been published. Poetry was the most preferred style of written expression of LTTE members. Short stories and short novels were also written. There were some good contributions to LTTE literature by female writers too. There were frequent book release functions during this period for books written by members and civilians. The CD releases were a lot more common, and they were almost always songs about military victories or about the death of an outstanding member.

Retailing: The food chain Paandiyan with a few outlets spread around Vanni created a culture of eating out and also generated a lot of revenue for the LTTE finance division. There were other food outlet centers, also operated by the finance division. In addition, there were several retail outlet chains for groceries and clothing. Although LTTE members were prohibited from drinking alcohol, the finance division also ran a chain of taverns for use by civilians. These commercial ventures by the LTTE must have generated a lot of income. Yet, it did not prevent private commercial activities, and there were many such private ventures, some of them very profitable. The LTTE did extract taxes from these private commercial operations. It also ran some manufacturing operations of dry food, plastic ware, and clothing for use by the local population. All of these ventures provided employment to thousands of civilians.

Valangkal: The finance division also operated many farms, including banana and poultry farms. I suspect that most of the produce from these farms went to feed LTTE members. The entire LTTE organization had a system called *valangkal* for providing the daily needs of its members. The prominent aspect of this was the provision of food. During lunch, I too ate the food provided by the *valangkal* system, and it was nutritious and tasty. Married LTTE families were also given a monthly income to run their homes.

Banking: The LTTE started its Bank in 1994 while it controlled Jaffna. But it grew in size in Vanni. The bank was used by the majority of the people in Vanni and it had several branches throughout the area. Especially after the ceasefire, the Diaspora was encouraged to deposit savings with the bank to assist in the growth of the region. It opened an impressive building for its headquarters in Kilinochchi only in 2008.

Fine arts: New schools of fine arts opened in two centers and taught full-time as well as after-school students. Many artists in painting, sculpture, and movie-making from Tamilnaadu came over to train students in various fields. NTT Television was launched and began broadcasting three to four hours a day during the evening. The skill of recording through electronic visual media had been developed within LTTE for decades. Thus, LTTE had a huge collection of video recordings, and NTT Television service started a project to maintain a well-categorized collection of the video recordings. The launch of NTT spurred a profusion of development in the visual media. Some notable full-length feature movies had already been made by LTTE prior to the ceasefire period. During the ceasefire period, great efforts were made to develop this further. The last of such movies, *Ellaalan*—on the attack on the Anuraathapuram Lankan Air Force base by twenty-two Black Tigers—was only partially completed by the time of the Kilinochchi displacement in late 2008. It was completed and released after the demise of the LTTE in May 2009.

Fitness: Karate was always popular among the LTTE as well as among civilians in the region. Efforts were made to facilitate every school-going child in attending karate training. Region-wide competitions were conducted for all age groups, and for both males and females. This was quite an astounding program for that part of the world. If it had been continued, I believe girls would have benefited the most from this program.

Documentation: Yogi Yogaratnam was in charge of an institution called Aavanakkaappakam, meaning "institution to protect documents". This institution documented military-related history. Yogi was among the hundreds of people who had disappeared after they were captured by the Lankan Military as they walked out of the war zone during the end war in 2009. There was another institution, Maaveerar kaappakam, which maintained the details of *maaveerar* and also was responsible for the upkeep of the many *thuyilum-illam*. The invaluable collection of books and documents were spread across Vanni, held in many institutions. For example, the Peace Secretariat itself had an excellent library of books on the subject of politics. Another institution, the Statistical Centre for North East (SNE), was formed which launched a massive homeland-wide project to collect war-related statistics.

Public transport: The only public transport available in Vanni was operated by the finance wing. It was efficient, affordable, and ran on time. I was told that prior to the ceasefire, 90 percent of the public transport in Vanni was provided by private mini-bus owners. Once the A9 route was opened following the signing of the ceasefire, fatal accidents caused by speeding vehicles jumped sharply. Private mini-buses providing public transport were the major culprits. This apparently forced the LTTE to move in to ban all privately owned public transport services.

Traffic: The clearly marked vehicles of the international agencies and the recognizable vehicles of the LTTE were mainly the ones that filled Vanni roads. Traffic through to Jaffna also filled the A9 road through Vanni. There were also the buses belonging to the public transport service of the LTTE. The ceasefire spurred an ever-growing number of motorcycles on the road. Other notable users of the major roads were the cows, goats, and dogs. Cows, especially, became a road hazard. Cows, both in ones and twos as well as large herds going to or returning from grazing, were major users of the roads. During the rainy season the center of the road was the only dry spot for many cows. Vehicles would just drive around the cows sitting in the center of the road. Until 2007, no effort was made to stop the cows claiming the right to use the roads as they were considered an important part of the economic life of Vanni. However, some effort was made to confiscate the cows, forcing the owners to make some efforts to keep them away from the busy roads.

Tamil Eelam police manning the Vanni roads to limit the speed of vehicles was a major topic of discussion in the public space. The people, having gotten used to no vehicles except the LTTE vehicles that were using the extremely poor roads during the pre-2002 war phase, needed to be re-educated on the importance of safety on the roads. There were indeed a large number of accidents soon after the ceasefire when the A9 road through Vanni was opened for through traffic north and south. Even pedestrians needed to relearn to walk on the sides of the road and not on the road itself. Vehicle drivers, both LTTE as well as those using the A9 as through traffic, thought speed limits in this region were not to be respected. LTTE drivers, having driven wildly during the war phase, found it very hard to limit their speed. The drivers of through traffic felt that no one could stop them speeding in this region. The Tamil Eelam traffic police did take stern action, and one could see the reduction of speeding vehicles as time passed.

A popular story retold at this time was a revised version of the tortoise and the hare story. The story goes like this. The hare, instead of falling asleep under a tree, was arrested by the Tamil Eelam police for speeding, thus giving a chance for the tortoise to win the race.

By mid-2006, however, this hive of activity suffered as the blockade was gradually re-imposed by the Lankan government.

15

The slow walk to Mullivaikaal

What I have described so far is what I have referred to in the title of this book as the "fleeting moment". What follows on the other hand is the process of the destruction of everything that I have described so far. Can the readers who did not experience this imagine what it is like to watch the complete destruction of one's country: the physical destruction, the destruction of the governance structures, the complete dispersal of its people, and massacres on a massive scale? Has there ever been such complete destruction of a country in history? The only reason why it is not seen as such is because my country was only in the minds of its people, but was not recognized by the global system of states.

Like everyone living in Vanni and the millions of Tamils world over, I experienced this pain. I will describe only what I experienced firsthand. Thus, what follows is only what I saw of a much wider phenomenon of war and human struggle. Most of us in Vanni at that time lived through it, unable to properly comprehend the impending destruction; totally incapable of thinking about the possibility that the existing de-facto state setup that was so extensive could be completely destroyed. As the LTTE lost more and more land area, a common refrain repeated in Vanni was that the Lankan army was spreading its legs too wide and it would meet its downfall in due course. Most of us believed it because we wanted to believe it. It was next to impossible to think of any other alternative. I was numbed when I first saw displacing people who did so with a smile as if they were going on a picnic. Unlike me, most of them had displaced several times before—prior to 2002—and took it in their stride. Until the start of 2009, the death toll within Vanni remained relatively low because people kept displacing out of the reach of the artillery fire. This also added to the upbeat mood of the people.

Even as late as January 2009, Pulitheevan commented, after browsing the web news, how Lanka was becoming confident of victory. When I responded saying everyone except the LTTE thinks that the Lanka military is winning, he just asked me if I wanted to leave. The impending calamity began its evolution from 2006 onwards, for almost three and a half years. Each year was colored by unfolding events of greater and greater magnitude.

2005

At the dawn of the year 2005, two dramatic events had taken place that altered the scene in Vanni: defection from the LTTE in April 2004 by the Batticaloa commander, Karunaa, and the 2004 Boxing Day tsunami. The shock waves caused by these events were already receding as 2005 unfolded. Indeed, there was some optimism about the Post Tsunami Operational Management Structure (PTOMS). This was an agreement drawn up by the Norwegian facilitators, which was independent of the earlier 2002 ceasefire agreement. Much of the frustration in Vanni caused by the lack of progress following the earlier stalled peace talks had also been put away, and the PTOMS was the talk of the town and the source of much hope. I attended a very large women's meeting called by the women's wing of the LTTE, to discuss a proposal aimed at channelling the PTOMS funds for benefiting women. The plan discussed was grandiose, and the main feature was a network of all-in-one offices that catered to the varying needs of women. It was exciting. PTOMS was signed in June 2005, but never came into existence because it was immediately challenged in the Lankan courts and was put on permanent hold. The failure of PTOMS to materialize broke all hope that there would be peace dividends for the Tamils.

It also seemed to me then that the defection of Karunaa had been taken in its stride by the Vanni establishment. After Karunaa's defection, violence in the eastern district of Batticaloa was on the rise and there were three high-profile murders of Tamils: freelance journalist Aiyaathurai Nadeesan and NESoHR founding member Chanthira Nehru, together with Batticaloa LTTE Political Head Kousalyan. During this time, well-known journalist Dharmaratnam Sivaram was assaulted in Batticaloa. After my arrival in Vanni, Sivaram was assassinated in Colombo in April 2005. The first high-profile assassination since the 2002 ceasefire for which the LTTE was blamed was that of Lankan foreign minister Lakshman Kadirgamar in August 2005. Soon after this, the LTTE issued a veiled call for the boycott of the presidential elections to be held in November 2005—the war-president was thus elected.

2006

The year began with increased levels of "white-van" abductions and killings. Victims' families visited NESoHR to report the incidents.

Several of the reports[17] I wrote for NESoHR resulted from such interviews with the affected families. I also helped produce a report, *White Van,*[18] on this phenomenon, based on the interviews we held at NESoHR.

It was against this background that the decision to hold direct talks in Geneva in February 2006 was made. During these peace talks the violence went down dramatically, and it was taken note of by the peacemakers as clearly indicating that both sides could control the violence if they chose to. The talks were a disappointment, the returning LTTE delegation received rough treatment at the Lankan international airport and violence flared up soon after. Starting from around this time, the entire adult Vanni population was put through a compulsory physical training routine by LTTE members. These were held during the early evenings, after the working day. One could see men and women with meter-long wooden logs on the roads heading to these training sessions at nearby open grounds. As batches completed these training sessions, there would be a training completion ceremony. The local television news would also carry news of these completion ceremonies. These training sessions were meant to increase the physical stamina of the people for an impending war.

The killing spree by death squads in Jaffna and Batticaloa reached a crescendo, and there were daily reports of a number of killings. There were also three high-profile attacks in Lanka, blamed on the LTTE that took the lives of nearly one hundred civilians in total. The largest of these attacks was on a bus in Kebitigollawa that killed sixty-eight civilians. I was never privy to discussions among LTTE members in Vanni about these attacks, except about what had already appeared in the media. These attacks appeared to take most LTTE members with whom I interacted on a regular basis also by surprise because they belonged to the political wing.

Until August 2006, the rising levels of violence seemed to all happen far away from Kilinochchi. In August, the violence arrived in Vanni, with the bombing of the Senchoolai complex in Vallipunam that killed more than fifty-four young female school students and injured more than 150. The effect of this bombing and the mayhem was felt deeply in Vanni. For a long time after, it kept coming up in conversations. Because it affected so many people, often references were made to people as one whose sister or daughter was killed or injured in the Senchoolai bombing. I did not personally know any of the girls affected in this bombing, though I met many of the survivors after the event. I also had an emotional connection to this complex, where I had stayed during my first visit when the Senchoolai children's home was functioning there. This is how the complex got its name. But there was no children's home operating there at the time of bombing. The complex was used just as a storehouse for the Senchoolai children's home. It was one of the half a dozen or so locations where week-long courses for senior school students, both boys and girls, were being conducted in August 2006. The workshops were a combined effort of the LTTE and the schools, but initiated and led by LTTE. Since very large numbers of senior students were attending the workshops, it was widely known, and there was no secrecy around it. Targeting this complex at this time would have been done with very clear knowledge of these facts.

There was indeed a military rationale for this attack. This community-wide leadership course was the culmination of several weeks of early morning physical training exercises held by the LTTE for senior school students prior to the start of the school day. Encouraging the senior students to join the LTTE was one of the motives. The students who participated in the in-house workshops were enthusiastic and made friendships with the LTTE members, and a large number from them would have willingly joined the movement. It was to stop this evolving development that the Senchoolai complex was bombed. As expected, this brought an immediate end to all the courses, and the psychological scar caused by it alienated many of the students who attended the course. In Vanni, many believed that if the courses had run to completion, there would not have been the forced recruitment practice that was put in place soon after this. August 2006 was packed with tragedies and military setbacks for the Tamils.

The Lankan Military launched a fully-fledged war in Trincomalee in August using the excuse of a trivial protest by Tamil farmers. The farmers shut a sluice gate which blocked irrigation water to farmlands in a Sinhala area. The gate was quickly opened with SLMM intervention, but the war continued. This war resulted in the LTTE defeat in Vaaharai by the end of 2006. The point-blank shooting of fourteen local employees of the French NGO, Action Contre Le Faim, in Trincomalee occurred during this month. More than 200 civilians were killed in the Lankan bombing and shelling in this war that ended in Vaaharai by the end of 2006. At the Peace Secretariat, we followed this war closely. The civilian deaths and the blockade of food were reported on the Peace Secretariat website. This pattern of herding civilians, imposing blockades, and bombing and shelling them was repeated in Vanni from 2007 onwards. For those of us who followed the Vaaharai war in 2006, the pattern was unmistakable as we were gradually herded into Mullivaikaal for the final massacre.

A lot of LTTE members walked back to Vanni from Trincomalee after the end of the war in Vaaharai. Some were even killed en route to Vanni. Notable among the arrivals was Elilan, the Trincomalee political head, whom I came to know well in Kilinochchi during 2007. He was a thoughtful person with a good understanding of the media, and would often point out the unbalanced nature of media reporting and give ideas on how to bring out issues that would provide some balance. He is another one of those missing, after capture by the Lankan Military as he walked out of the war zone with his family during the end war in 2009.

In the same month of August, parallel to the Vaaharai war, another war also erupted in Muhamalai along the northern border of Vanni. The LTTE faced another serious setback but these clashes did not flare up into a continuing war at that time. Lankan shelling of the Allaipiddy church, on an islet off the Jaffna coast, also took the lives of an unknown number of civilians. Efforts by the church priest, Fr. Jim Brown, to evacuate the injured civilians were blocked by the Lankan Navy. Fr. Jim Brown also disappeared during this month. There was also a claymore attack on a clearly marked ambulance vehicle in Vanni, which took the lives of the doctor, nurse, and three more civilians in the vehicle.

Also in the month of August, a Lankan Peace Secretariat official, Kethees Loganathan, was shot and killed in Colombo, allegedly by the LTTE.

In 2006, sandwiching these horrendous events, two direct talks between the Lankan government and LTTE were held in Geneva, at the insistence of the peace makers. The second of the two 2006 Geneva talks took place in October. The October Geneva talks were a non-event in Vanni. Anton Balasingkam, who led the 2006 February talks, could not attend the October talks due to his deteriorating health. Thamilselvan led the LTTE delegation. The reopening of the A9 road, which was closed in August, was the topic that the LTTE kept pushing. The peacemakers tried valiantly to fix another date for talks. Citing the ceasefire agreement on keeping the A9 road open, the LTTE would not agree on another date for talks until the A9 road was reopened. The Lankan government failed to do this. Thus, the 2006 October talk was the very last direct talks based on the 2002 ceasefire agreement. On return, Thamilselvan never tired of discussing these talks, which were led by him. He was full of confidence as always.

The death of Anton Balasingkam in December 2006 brought to the fore the deep love and respect he had earned among LTTE members. Though I never interacted with him, I came to know more about him through the affection members expressed in casual interactions during that period of mourning.

2007

The struggle for fuel and the death of Thamilselvan stand as markers for the year 2007 in Vanni. Every sector of life in Vanni struggled with the fuel shortage. I faced frustrations all around due to the fuel shortage. In my work in releasing underage persons from the LTTE, we also needed to convince UNICEF of the releases. We faced problems with visiting the families in order to confirm the releases due to fuel shortage. At the same time, UNICEF faced problems travelling to border areas due to security restrictions. Many releases were unacknowledged by UNICEF due to this. Even updating the LTTE website with the latest attacks on civilians was delayed due to fuel issues. There were endless accusations and counter accusations between Thamilselvan and the media unit that was supposed to provide the news. Thamilselvan would never accept lack of fuel as an excuse for non-reporting, while the media personnel felt under-resourced.

The common mode of transport in Vanni at this time was motorbikes. As the price of petrol became exorbitant, people converted their motorbikes to run on kerosene, which was relatively cheaper. The technology to do this had already been perfected during the previous decades of war. The conversion involved an open-ended tube that led to the engine's carburetor. To start the motorbike running on kerosene, a droplet of petrol was fed through the tube, and the driver then blew into the tube to provide more oxygen. The blowing into the tube would be continued at regular intervals while riding, which must have damaged their lungs. It was a common sight on the streets of Vanni at this time that symbolized the struggle of the people against the Lankan government that sadistically imposed tighter and tighter fuel restrictions.

Massacres by aerial bombing had become a very common occurrence by then. 2007 was launched with the second largest civilian attack in Vanni since the ceasefire. On 2 January, a tiny fishing village, Padahuthurai, was bombed, killing fifteen members of an extended family, including five preschoolers. I helped produce a report, *Kfir Fodder*,[19] on this based on eyewitness interviews. Immediately after this attack, and in the same month, there were two large-scale attacks on civilian vehicles in Lanka for which LTTE stood accused. These were in Nitambuwa and Peraliya, and took the lives of twenty-two civilians. The year was saturated with killings and disappearances in the Tamil homeland by the Lankan-sponsored paramilitary groups. Around 500 such deaths and another 500 disappearances were recorded by us at the Peace Secretariat.

The disparity in national and international reporting on the civilian deaths in the two regions, the Tamil homeland and Lanka, was so stark for those who were following the events so closely. It was to counter this imbalance that the LTTE appointed a spokesperson on human rights in 2007, but that did not change the imbalance. Understanding this imbalance using the Chomsky-Herman propaganda model is useful. The three important filters proposed in their model were, ownership of media, advertisers' influence on the media, and how the news was sourced by the media. As we closely observed the imbalance in the reporting of each event in the two regions—the Tamil homeland and Lanka—we could observe several sub-filters through which news was filtered before reaching the outside. This news would then be further filtered by the Chomsky-Herman filters, resulting in a rather unbelievable level of disparity in the reporting of civilian casualties in the Tamil homeland. The ground level filters we identified could be grouped into three main categories: fear filter, resource filter, and center-of-gravity filter.

During 2007, death squads were operating in Tamil areas under Lankan control with total impunity. Frequent murders of journalists and attacks on the media institutions made this *fear filter* very effective. Ordinary people were too scared to speak. Even priests who dared to speak were not spared. The disappearance of Fr. Jim Brown in 2006 was just one well-known case.

The second filter operating was the *resource filter*. The resource availability was a crucial element determining how much information—in a format palatable to the outside world—is conveyed. To achieve effective information transfer, fuel availability, English language, computer skills, and communication facilities were crucial. That there was a huge disparity in this aspect between the two parties goes without saying. The blockade imposed by the Lankan government on Vanni sharpened this imbalance even further.

The third filter that was operating was the *center-of-gravity filter*. All international agencies, including diplomatic missions, the SLMM head office, UN agencies, and the bureaus of the international news wire services, were located in Colombo. Although some of these international agencies had representatives in the Tamil areas, their head offices in Colombo invariably had the power to overrule these representatives. Thus, these bodies ended up having greater contact with, and were greatly influenced by, the Lankan government. In addition, journalists were often blocked from going to the location of an incident in the Tamil areas to do their own investigation. All of this created a heavy bias towards the Lankan version of events among these bodies.

At the Peace Secretariat, where until this time there was all-day electricity provided by locally run generators, it was now limited to only a few hours during the day. I was left with many hours to spend without electricity. Teaching a class of new recruits in the political division also was an enjoyable diversion from the deteriorating working conditions. These classes were made up of new recruits under the strict one per family recruitment policy. Some of the more academically able were selected for study. These classes were separate for boys and girls. Thamilselvan took personal interest in their education, and they were given excellent facilities in which to concentrate on their studies. The initial focus of their education was the English language. Many of us took classes in English and it was ably coordinated by a member from Thamilselvan's innermost squad. The teachers did not have much interaction with each other, but the coordinator made sure that we were not duplicating. I mixed a lot of my alternative views on the world with teaching English, and all of us, the students and I, enjoyed it. The young people showed no sign that they were recruited under a compulsory scheme. They were all dedicated to the LTTE cause and willingly discussed issues freely. It was difficult not become attached to such a group of young people. All of them were sent to battle and many died.

A small-scale concrete bomb shelter was built in the Peace Secretariat grounds, but we sought protection there only on a handful of occasions, preferring instead to move out to the playground nearby and watch the bombers diving down. Thamilselvan remained confident that the Peace Secretariat would not be bombed.

The bombing of Thamilselvan's office/residence in the middle of Kilinochchi in the early morning of 2 November 2007 was up to that time the nearest I had been to such an explosion. There were many more as time went by where I came even closer to bombing incidents than this. My residence at the time of the bombing of Thamilselvan's office/residence was on the A9 road, and it was less than a kilometer from his place. Before it was publicly announced, people openly wept and shared the news among each other. After the news broke out, a gloomy stillness pervaded the place. His assassination touched a very deep nerve in the people in Vanni, and it was forcefully demonstrated during his funeral. During the last few hours of his funeral, his body was in the Cultural Hall on the A9 road, very close to where I lived at the CWDR hostel. The crowd filled the street and all the surrounding land. I could hear the speeches from my room. The Lankan bombers kept sweeping down creating that frightening noise; a noise which always sends everyone running for cover in the bunkers. On this occasion no one moved and that message from the crowd was clearly heard by everyone. This was the same man who instituted the forced recruitment and earned much outrage from the people as a result. It is as if by giving his life, he had washed away all that anger.

Many of his compatriots had urged him, prior to his assassination, to shift his office/residence for safety. A new office/residence for him had already been built and was ready for use, but Thamilselvan procrastinated from moving there, partly due to his confidence that the Peace Secretariat and his office/residence would be spared because they were the centers of an internationally facilitated ceasefire agreement and peace process that still had some official currency.

Thamilselvan's intelligence, dedication, and qualities of leadership were outstanding. He had the ability to direct meetings. He held frequent meetings with people on wide- ranging topics. Besides LTTE members, expatriate international NGO staff, religious leaders, and Lankan government employees met him regularly. Even if there were sharp disagreements during his meetings, he managed them well and they were always harmonious. On a greater scale, he managed a massive sub-organization of various branches of the political division brilliantly. He appeared to spread a warm Thamilselvan space around him, within which everyone felt comfortable working. Both LTTE members and non-members alike kind of swam in it, and it was always good to seek his view. It was more than his intelligence and competence that helped create this aura. It was his truly selfless service. Western media writing about him after his death said he was the public face of the LTTE; a smiling rebel cum de-facto prime minister. I wrote an obituary for him where I said,

> *"I learnt something about the renowned LTTE member*
> *view of the world talking to Thamilselvan. It was not*
> *said directly, but he—in a very literal sense—did not*
> *fear death. He contributed to my understanding of*
> *how ready and fearless they are to die. ..."*

In Kilinochchi, his absence was deeply felt. Some members would always be in tears when they spoke of him. All the institutions that came under his authority also missed his leadership. People never stopped referring back to him when problems arose. My line of work at the Peace Secretariat was affected, too, by his demise, and I also felt a great sense of loss. Others whom I knew too felt the ripple effect of his demise long after.

November 2007 Maaveerar Day arrived within three weeks of Thamilselvan's demise. As the climax of the Maaveerar Day commemoration approached, Lankan bombers flew over the Vanni skies attempting to frighten the people. The Voice of Tiger radio station on the A9 road in Kilinochchi was bombed, killing many people working there as well as many civilians walking on the A9 road in front of it. We were at the Peace Secretariat waiting to update the website of the day's event. It was clear that it was not safe to be at the Peace Secretariat, and I was asked to wait at the SLMM Kilinochchi office for my own safety.

2008

The dawn of 2008 saw the official abrogation of the 2002 ceasefire agreement by the Lankan government, which by then only existed on paper. It still created a big vacuum in Vanni because the SLMM office was closed and all the SLMM officers had left. With the abrogation of the ceasefire agreement, the Peace Secretariat did not hold any official position. By this time there had already been several aerial attacks in Kilinochchi, and thus the Peace Secretariat lost all pretense of being a safe place.

A residential house belonging to some local government authority was hijacked to be used as the new Peace Secretariat, from which some of us could work. Attempts were made to keep this a secretive location. Because my residence was also now deemed unsafe, I began to live and work in this hijacked building from January 2008. Just a handful of Peace Secretariat employees and members worked there, and I missed the frequent interactions one had with the many and varied people who used to visit the old Peace Secretariat. The isolation was an unpleasant necessity so that I need not run to the bomb shelter at all times during the day and night whenever the noise of a bomber could be heard. It was also due to this reason that I had very minimal interactions with the new political head, Nadeesan. Though Nadeesan maintained the minimum age limit of eighteen recruitment policy, I felt that his approach to it was lukewarm compared to the stance Thamilselvan had taken. I felt disappointed about the progress of this project.

The incessant aerial bombings and claymore attacks had become part of our lives now. But fuel shortage meant reporting about them was also a struggle. I helped produce two more video documentaries on two incidents in January and February 2008. One was, *Madhu Amma,*[20] on a claymore attack on a bus with school children near Madhu church. The other was about a bombing attack on the village of Kiranchi. In this attack, following the first bombing attack as people were removing the injured and the dead from the scene, the bomber returned and bombed the same spot again. We therefore called this documentary, *Bomber Returned.*[21] In Vanni, such repeated bombing of the same spot just few minutes apart with the intention of killing those clearing the scene occurred often.

I seriously considered leaving Vanni around this time, but fear of crossing the Lankan Military checkpoint made me hesitate. There was already a report of a Tamil Diaspora member going missing at the checkpoint. In April 2008 came the shocking news of the assassination of NESoHR chairperson, Kili-father. Even before recovering from the news, I realized that I had my work cut out for me as a result of his death. I had not involved myself directly with NESoHR work from around May 2006 because of my involvement with the Peace Secretariat. I knew I would now be called upon to take an active role within NESoHR. I was asked to step into his shoes by Pulitheevan, which I resisted, saying I could not take that role because I was not a citizen of Sri Lanka.

From this time onwards until displacement from Kilinochchi in October, I was busy writing NESoHR reports on many and varied topics. Ramanan, the NESoHR coordinator, was a tireless worker who helped me to gather information on all the varied topics on which we released reports. Food shortages and medicine shortages were starting to hit Vanni by now due to restrictions at the checkpoint, and NESoHR released several reports on this situation. People expressed confidence that people would not starve in Vanni because Vanni was an agricultural area. This confidence started to break down as produce from many of the agricultural lands were lost as people evacuated. The milk powder shortage was felt sharply because the majority of the people depended on milk powder as their main source of milk. All Vanni institutions offered tea with milk powder to their employees during the morning and afternoon. Offering tea to visitors was one of the established practices, and even offices were following this tradition. Now, instead of milk tea, everyone was offered black tea. It became harder to buy medicines privately in the shops. I knew many asthma sufferers who struggled to obtain asthma inhalers. I, too, suffered from a lack of asthma medication.

By this time, deaths of LTTE members known to me started to occur at regular frequency. One death in particular, of a female member, Vasanthi, moved me deeply. She regularly gave me transport on her motorbike. Just a few days before she was killed by enemy shelling, she wrote to me from the front line. Vasanthi was from Batticaloa, and she had joined the LTTE a few years earlier to avenge the killing of her civilian brother by the Lankan Military. She was to marry a fellow fighter, Thabethan. A few weeks after her death, Thabethan too was killed on the front line. How do people deal with such repeated losses? Mourning for the loss of a loved one, I thought, is like a sore on the skin. It scabs over and then becomes normal. When the skin is repeatedly injured it takes on a more permanent hardness. That is what it felt like when I attended funerals of those known to me with increased frequency. Some part of the heart hardens in order to deal with the pain.

I attended many of these LTTE funerals. Every such funeral had a long ceremony to make sure everyone who knew the fallen member had a chance to pay tribute. The body was embalmed by an LTTE division. The aim of embalming was to keep the body presentable for a few days while the final rites were performed. The embalmed body was first placed at the home of the fallen member for two or three days. Two LTTE members always stood guard and an extra marquee was erected around the house for the expected visitors. In the final journey, the body was taken to a public hall, where those known to the fallen member would give speeches. Finally the body would take its final journey to the *thuyilum-illam*. There would be another long ritual there on a large stage, where LTTE members would stand to attention and give their final salute. Family and friends would stand around wailing and crying for their loved one. The body was then taken to the already prepared hole in the ground and would be lowered into it. Everyone would then throw a handful of soil on the coffin before it was finally covered. Then family and friends were given tea or a soft drink while seated under the trees, exhausted. A framed picture of the fallen member, covered in the LTTE flag, would be handed to the closest kin present by a senior member before the family was bid farewell from the *thuyilum-illam*. It was an exhaustingly long ceremony and somehow also acted as an effective grieving process. One left with the impression that the *maaveerar* was indeed resting there.

It was in this besieged atmosphere in September 2008 that the Lankan order came to the international agencies in Vanni to vacate the area. Several people said to me at that time that this was a precursor to the impending genocide. I met the UNICEF head in Kilinochchi to discuss the ongoing program on child soldiers. I expressed my concerns about their not clearing up the UNICEF list of child soldiers. Probably unwittingly, he said that was the least of their concerns at that moment. We met another UN official just before they left Kilinochchi at the NESoHR office. She told us they would be back in three months, and I naively believed it. People protested at the UN office in Kilinochchi, pleading with them not to leave. People even blockaded the convoy of vehicles that were ready to leave. The protest delayed their departure by a day or two, and with that all international observers, except the ICRC, left Vanni. In fact the Lankan government ordered the ICRC out, too, but the ICRC stood its ground only to suffer shell attacks directly on its displaced location later.

Within weeks of the departure of the UN, in the beginning of October 2008, Kilinochchi was evacuated. The thoroughness and organized manner in which people and institutions in Kilinochchi evacuated was very impressive. During the short interval of peace from 2002-2006, people had spent their resources to build up homes and offices, and they were not prepared to abandon all that. So almost everyone set about dismantling everything they could, including the roofing of their homes and offices, and took it away with them. It was a massive operation that used up the manpower of the entire Kilinochchi population. Indeed, one of the journalists who was taken to Kilinochchi, by the Lankan Military, after it had fallen, wrote that he could not find even a piece of paper left behind by the evacuating people.

The majority of the Kilinochchi people set themselves up in Tharmapuram, unwilling to move any further away from Kilinochchi, and with the expectation to return to Kilinochchi in a few months. Tharmapuram thus became a new satellite town of abandoned Kilinochchi. The streets were extremely crowded. For the Hindu Deepavali festival that came soon after the displacement, makeshift shops in Tharmapuram displayed a wide array of clothing and other goods at bargain prices. In fact, many of the retailers were trying to unload their stock rather than having to cart it every time they displaced. Travelling through Tharmapuram during this time, one could sense the community feeling of a people struggling together against great odds.

For nearly five months until late February 2009, I stayed at the Senthalir children's home in Vallipunam, which was run by the CWDR. For the first month I just ate and slept, having no access to electricity or internet. Ramanan did an excellent job of setting up a new NESoHR office in Puthukkudiyiruppu, and a Peace Secretariat office was also set up in Vallipunam, not far from Senthalir, where I stayed.

During November and December of 2008, with the new NESoHR office at Puthukkudiyiruppu and the internet facilities provided by the new Peace Secretariat office in Vallipunam, we produced more reports, as best as we could, amid the aerial bombings. One of the reports I wrote for NESoHR at this time was about an incident where cluster bombs used by Lankan Military on civilian targets.[22] Other Tamil media channels also reported it. Yet, as usual, the international agencies refused to report this news on the use of a banned weapon.

In December 2008, I faced the first close call in an aerial bombing near Senthalir. As the noise of the bomber got closer and louder, I walked out of my room towards the bunker. I heard several shrapnel pieces falling just behind me. Later we collected dozens of shrapnel pieces in the yard of the children's home. These are very sharp metal pieces that were too hot to touch soon after an explosion. If a piece touched the body it was sure to maim or kill.

The one per family recruitment policy of LTTE appeared to have stabilized once it had exhausted this option. The losses on the front lines, however, meant that the LTTE faced a severe manpower shortage. The LTTE started to demand voluntary services from civilians to do many tasks on the front lines that did not have direct military involvement, such as cooking and digging trenches. The recruitment efforts thus shifted to persuading people to give up their time. It was always the males who were subjected to this, and if they survived the Lankan artillery attacks during their time on the front lines, they did return back to their families in a few weeks. People discussed not the fact that they were taken away for one-month-long compulsory work near the front lines, but the manner in which some were just dragged away from roads and other places without adequate warning. Some of them died in Lankan artillery fire and aerial bombing while at front line, and this was also the reason for the growing anger. I spoke to the LTTE members involved in the task of persuading civilians to perform non-military duties near the front lines. The members I knew performed this task in a civilized manner, and indeed many men willingly gave their time. Sadly, among them, some died of artillery attack while on the front line.

Great efforts were made to ensure that the Maaveerar Day of 2008 was celebrated as grandly as possible, but the mood by then among civilians was somber and not enthusiastic. However, I noticed the same religious devotion to attend Maaveerar Day among mothers and families of *maaveerar*. There was heavy rain, and buses could not cross many of the flooded roads. Families walked through floods for miles in order to be at the *thuyilum-illam* for Maaveerar Day.

We saw a 2008 Christmas display in a church, whose creators clearly wanted to give hope to the people. It had quotes from the Bible. One of the Peace Secretariat staff brought a photo of it and it was posted it on the website. One of its Biblical quotes read:

> *"You will cry and mourn. The world will rejoice at that.*
> *You will be saddened by it. But your misery will transform*
> *into great joy."*

2009

By January 2009 we were well set up with new offices for NESoHR at Puthukkudiyiruppu, and the Peace Secretariat at Vallipunam. Only in January, the Peace Secretariat in Vallipunam completed a bunker facility.

I was busy with my report on the 1990s expulsion of people from the villages of Kokkilaay-Kokkuththoduvaay-Karunaaddukkeeni, almost enjoying it despite the atmosphere. There was chaos on the roads in January 2009, as a new wave of displacement was taking place. People Tharmapuram, the most crowded area in Vanni, was now on the move following several artillery attacks on it.

In January, the Lankan government declared its first "safe zone" for civilians. Senthalir, where I was staying, was on the Paranthan-Mullaithithu road, along which ran the border of the first "safe-zone". There was discussion on whether Senthalir fell inside or outside this "safe zone". One LTTE woman dismissed the discussions, saying that the "safe zone" was a farce. I was a little confused at that time. How right she was. She had judged the "safe zone" with so much clarity.

On 22 January, I was at the Vallipunam Peace Secretariat office when the shelling started. We all crowded into the just-completed bunker. The noise of the explosions was so loud that we could not hear each other talk. One NESoHR employee, who was at the newly located Mullaithiivu hospital in the Vallipunam school ground, came rushing, bruised and with his pants torn. His camera was full of pictures of the artillery attack on this newly located hospital. From that day onwards, artillery noise was loud, and getting out on the road was taking a gamble with one's life. There were many deaths of civilians around us. Everyone on the road was nervous, and yet the roads were now getting more and more crowded with the number of people on the move was on the rise again. One couple from the Peace Secretariat, Selvi and Bavan, were seriously injured during this time as they attempted to displace with their baby on motorbike. Bavan, who had lost a leg in battle many years ago, was now joined by his wife Selvi, who also lost a leg as a result of this latest injury.

I did not go to the NESoHR office after this. I made one more trip to the Peace Secretariat office. Foolishly, I left my laptop there that night and it was lost forever with all my data. What I miss most from my laptop is the nearly completed Kokkilaay-Kokkuththoduvaay-Karunaaddukeeni report. For two weeks I stayed in my room at Senthalir, listening to shells whizzing past and often going under the bed because I disliked staying in the crowded bunkers with screaming children. By then Senthalir was overcrowded with women and children from other CWDR centers also taking refuge. Everyone was busy building more bunkers. Around mid-February, Pulitheevan asked me to move into his temporary shelter, which was a little further away from the main road.

Puli would hardly be there, dropping in only for one night in a week. I was with his wife, Kurinchi. There were three or four other families, who had their tents in the same yard. We shared the well and one toilet. I had by this time told Puli that I wanted to leave, and he said he would make arrangements for it. A week or two after I moved out of Senthalir, the entire CWDR group of women and children at Senthalir evacuated to Suthanthirapuram. There, in one shell attack, a child was killed and three more were badly injured. I learnt of this much later because going to see them was out of the question at that stage. Listening to shells whizzing past had become the pastime for all of us. We got up from bed many times during the night to run to the bunker, which was already overcrowded with those sleeping in it.

Eventually Kurinchi and I had a bunker for ourselves, and we also started sleeping in it. Within a week or so of gaining this bunker facility, we had to displace yet again. On the last day of our stay in this place, I think it was somewhere between 17-22 February, the shelling was too heavy, and several strangers—men, women, and children—came into our bunker for shelter, saying their area nearby had been hit hard and some people had already been killed.

That day I displaced with Kurinchi and the other families to Iranaipaalai. All of us were advised to ensure that our motorbikes would not stall on a dangerous bit of road and to go at high speed without stopping for anyone while on this road. As our motorbikes sped along this road for about 6-7 minutes, all the way along I saw the decaying carcasses of cows, goats, and dogs killed by shelling. I was at Iranaipaalai for two weeks, but then I was with the family of another friend. This location was no better than the one we left behind. We faced constant artillery fire. Once someone handed me a large and heavy 25cm-long curved piece of shrapnel that had just fallen in the next yard seconds earlier. I dropped it immediately because it was too hot to hold.

At Iranaipaalai, in the same yard where I stayed with my friend's family, the staff of the head of political division Nadeesan had set up an internet facility. In this new location Nadeesan's staff was busy sending the latest videos of civilian massacres which were taking place all around us. A lot of effort was spent sending videos to Indian media outlets. One needed to be very agile to work in that environment, where one had to be ever vigilant of artillery fire and aerial bombers and be quick to seek shelter in a bunker. I was asked to work there, and though I tried to work in that environment, I could not because it was impossible to relax for a moment and concentrate on working. I made contact with my family in New Zealand from the internet facility and informed them I would be leaving Vanni soon.

I met Nadeesan for the last time in this place. Nadeesan and Pulitheevan were the two senior-most leaders executed in Mullivaikaal in May 2009 as they attempted to surrender to the Lankan army, following long-distance negotiations with the peace makers.[23]

While at this location, a female LTTE friend decided to take me around on her motorbike to show me the area. We travelled up to Maaththalan and back. The dirt roads were chaotic with pedestrians, motorbikes, and trucks. Along the road people were selling things in tiny shops, which were either a bench under a tree or a tarpaulin on the ground. People were living in tents along the beach that were unbearably hot. Mothers with babies sought whatever tiny piece of shade they could find. Some were taking shelter under trucks. We passed one truck loaded with dead bodies.

We moved from Iranaipaalai to Mullivaikaal around the beginning of March. The exact dates had by then become irrelevant, as we lived in the constant shadow of shelling and bombing. There was not a moment when one could relax without having one's ears glued to the noise of either shell explosions or the noise of bombers flying. When the sounds appeared too close, we had to seek shelter in whatever bunker was available. There were many families living in tents around us. Many of them were with very young children, and yet they dreaded ending up in the hands of the Lankan Military.

LTTE recruiters were now targeting everyone of fighting age who was not married, and the one per family policy had been abandoned. In one tent, when they came to recruit, the mother started to scream, but the young girl quietly walked over and got into their vehicle to be driven off. Another day, another young man was taken away from the yard adjacent to ours very early in the morning. We heard the wailing mother for a long time after.

I met the mother of a member who had just lost her son in battle. I had taught this boy in the English classes. He had been a long-term member and had been at battles before. He was then pulled from battle duty and brought to learn English. In 2008, the English classes were dissolved, and everyone was sent to front line duties. I met this particular student for the last time in mid-2008 on the road. He approached me and said he had been put on recruitment duty, and he was deeply upset and said he would prefer to be on the front line instead.

Around this time I heard for the first time rumors that the LTTE was shooting at people who were trying to cross over to the Lankan side. It was very depressing news. Later, in Manik Farm internment camp, some people in my camp, who were those who crossed during the month of March 2009, talked with outrage about being shot at as they crossed over to the Lankan side. Their assumption was that it was the LTTE who shot at them.

By now, the last rites of members were as low key as possible. I never went to any such last rite event after leaving Kilinochchi. Having lost all the land that had *thuyilum-illams,* new temporary ones were created to bury the fallen. For the civilian funerals, which were by now as common as LTTE funerals, the last rites were almost non-existent, like the only one that I attended near my tent in Mullivaikaal.

While in Mullivaikaal for three weeks in March, we learnt of several incidents that occurred within 200 meters of my tent in which civilians were hit by shells and killed. One particular incident I experienced directly. I cannot remember the exact date, but I think it was a week to ten days before I left Vanni on 20 March. I was sitting at the entrance to the tent when I saw a bright flash of light just three meters ahead of me. Instinctively I fell to the ground and the noise then reached us. The explosions appeared to go on for several minutes. When the noise paused long enough, all of us dashed to the bunker facility nearby where many people had crowded. I was too nervous to get out, but some did.

A 60-year-old man, Muthulingam, in the adjacent tent was killed as a shell hit his head while he was eating his lunch. A teenage girl in another tent near ours received severe abdominal injuries. We knew these two souls well because we met them regularly at the well. We also saw them frequently around the tents, as they were very close to ours. We heard that three more civilians, including a baby, were killed in the tents thirty meters away.

Within a few minutes of the attack, a vehicle belonging to the TRO arrived and picked up the bodies of the dead and the injured. The dead bodies were cleaned and brought back within an hour. Inside a neighbor's tent, which was still standing after the attack, old Muthulingam's body was laid on a bench. About ten people stood around while the dead man's wife cried. Someone sang some religious hymns, and an hour later the TRO vehicle came again to take the body. Some men in the neighborhood also drove away in the vehicle to help dig the hole to bury the body.

I met Puli after this incident and learnt that he too had been somewhere nearby and had had to crawl his way to a makeshift bunker. He sounded very dejected when he said that the Lankan Military did not appear to have any conscience, shelling directly on civilians like that. To me he appeared to believe that this type of incessant, blatant shelling directly in civilian areas was improbable and could not continue. It was possible that even the LTTE leadership counted on the improbability of such blatant shelling of civilian areas continuing for long.

Around this time I received permission to leave by ICRC ship. I had been waiting for this for nearly three months. On 19 March, I went to Maaththalan with the view to catching the ship. Along the way, in one spot a tent was shredded and there were blood stains. There had been a shell attack on the spot two days earlier. The ship was delayed and I waited in the Mullaithiivu District Secretariat, which by now was just a 4x4 meter shed with no walls. One side was stacked with sandbags. I was told the shells came from that end. The District Secretariat staff was there waiting. Their major task now was to appeal to the outside for food and receive it whenever it arrived by ICRC ship at this spot. While waiting, we heard the spreading news that there was an attack nearby. One man, whose family tent was in that area, immediately rushed to the spot and returned thirty minutes later saying that his family was safe, but there had been some deaths. I returned to Mullivaikaal because the passenger ship did not arrive that day. The next day I managed to catch the ship and arrived in Pulmooddai around 7.00 p.m.

15

The internment camps

On arrival at Pulmooddai by ICRC ship, we were entirely in the hands of the Lankan Navy. They began herding us like animals straight away. Eventually we were put on buses to take us to the final destination, Manik Farm in Vavuniya. The 100km journey took over three days and two nights in buses with standing space only. Many of the older people on the buses wailed and fainted. The first night we slept crowded together in a community hall in Pathaviya, and the second night at Omanthai on rough ground without adequate toilets. In between, we were interrogated several times, photographed, fingerprinted, and baggage checked down to a minute level. The repeated questioning by the Lankan navy, police, and military was clearly aimed at making us criticize the LTTE and praise the Lankan forces. Exhausted, we arrived at Manik Farm camp at midday on the third day. It took the rest of the day before we could seek shelter inside a hot tent allocated to us. The toilets were unfinished. Many of us drank water not meant for consumption and immediately had diarrhea. The struggle for shade from the hot sun, decent toilets, drinking water, washing water, and food continued throughout my stay. Each day, obtaining everything was a struggle, with so many people competing for the limited resources. In due course, illness afflicted everyone.

The camps were run by the Lankan Military, with civilian officers taking orders from them. The military, with batons or guns in hand, treated all of us like criminals. The military did not hesitate to use them to beat men and women and even the elderly. When the military were angered, they liberally used their boots, too, to attack the people. No one dared complain about the military excesses. Sometimes, when a Sinhala cabinet minister visited the camp, the convoy of Sinhala video teams that came with him would throw food at the people and then video with amusement as the people scrambled for the food that fell on the ground. I was interned for four months in this infamous Manik Farm with the 300,000 people who walked out of the war zone. The struggle to get out of this hellhole occupied all our minds constantly.

During those four months in the camp, it was the condition of the children at the camp that I found most depressing. I was too timid to go around collecting statistics, though it would have been easy because of the proximity of the people crowded within a small area. However, I observed carefully and was overwhelmed by the wasting away of the children. I kept telling myself how lucky I was that I did not have young children under my care.

Take the eight-tent group where I was staying. Five of the tents out of the eight had children under ten. One child died, one became seriously ill and was taken away to Vavuniya hospital, and all the other children had frequent fever, vomiting and diarrhea. Some of the children had persistent skin disease despite several visits to the doctors and treatment. Four of the children contracted Hepatitis A, and the parents were told by the doctors to just take good care of them and give them lots of fruit because the hospitals had no medicine. Fruit was very expensive in the camp. There was a native treatment for Hepatitis A involving a plant named *Keelkkaainelli* in Tamil. Even to get this plant was a struggle because it meant someone had to bring it from outside and hand over to the inmates at the inmate meeting spot, as described later.

Newborn babies were sent from hospitals, just a few days after being born, into the camp conditions, which were unsuitable even for adults. Toddlers played in the filthy area right in front of the toilets. I had never seen flies and mosquitoes in such numbers in my life. While eating, one hand was fully occupied with chasing the flies; a practice that children would not adopt, thus consuming food contaminated by flies that came straight from the toilets very nearby.

The majority of the children, including infants, did not have milk (powder) except an occasional packet handed out by some charity. Once, a father of a seven-month-old baby came begging for some sugar to put in the plain tea (black tea) to be given to his seven month old baby because the mother did not have enough breast milk and the baby was hungry. Plain tea had become the regular diet for this baby. The diet was most definitely inadequate for the children, despite some nutritional supplements that were distributed by some international agency. There was no milk, meat or vegetable in their diets. Sometimes soya beans were given, but they were of rotten quality, and the children would hardly eat them.

Illness among the children was pandemic, and they were wasting away. Small injuries became infected and caused problems. Vomiting, fever or diarrhea seemed a natural condition in most children. When a child ran a fever, most parents worried a lot, fearing Hepatitis A infection. Measures of malnutrition may be a standard way of measuring the worst-affected children, but it does not capture the general condition of children wasting away. Children who appeared well cared for on arrival at the camp were visibly wasting away during their stay. There were many contributory factors to their wasting away, but most of the physical factors, such as poor diet and exposure to hostile weather, had also existed for several months in Vanni prior to the period at Manik Farm. Yet, the children wasted away faster and suffered more illness in the internment camps. This only reinforced the well-known principle of the importance of the psychological well-being of the family and society for healthy child development.

The queues were very long at the medical clinics inside the camp, and doctors worked at breakneck speed. I saw a doctor writing a prescription for a twelve-year-old boy without finding out what was wrong first. The medicines that were dispensed were arranged on a table that had about thirty different medicines. The medicine dispensers, too, worked at breakneck speed in dispensing them. Once, an educated mother told me that she visited the doctor for treatment for her baby as well as for herself. The medicine dispensers mixed up the medicines and gave the baby what should have been given to the mother. Since the mother had some awareness of the medications, she spotted it. Most mothers in the camp, who did not have such awareness, would have given the adult medication to the baby. God only knows how many babies, children, and even adults died due to such medical negligence. Who was there in the camp to watch, monitor, and investigate? Perhaps the most telling scenes of the camp conditions and the health service could be found by visiting the medical clinics and observing young mothers with very sick babies in their hands waiting for a long time in queues with tears trickling down their faces.

Children went to makeshift schools staffed by teachers who were also interned in the camp. Many teachers lamented how it was impossible to teach while living under such conditions. The school was made up of sheds with uneven floors covered with tarpaulins. The children could not even place their books on the uneven floor to write. They had to keep the soft cover books on their knees to write.

Most of the young children had to carry very heavy buckets of water to assist their parents, who were also struggling to care for the children, often as a single parent. The weight, bending their little bodies like a question mark, surely would have done permanent damage.

Family separation, caused by many factors, was yet another ordeal that affected the camp community. Hundreds of injured people were taken by ICRC ship throughout the war period from Vanni. Often an adult family member, and sometimes young children who had no other caregiver left, accompanied the injured. The injured person and the accompanying family members were separated within a day or two of arrival, and the family members were taken to the camps, while the injured were sent away to some hospital. I knew family after family desperately trying, without much assistance from any authorities, to locate the injured family member, who could have been transferred to any number of the hospitals. Many a tearful month was spent by these families not knowing anything about the fate of their injured family member. Reunions of the injured with the family in many cases took place purely by the efforts of the family, with next to no help from the authorities.

The war conditions and the eventual escape from the war zone also separated families. Often while escaping, part of the family would cross over to the Lankan side, while the others failed to cross over. Again, many families wrote dozens of letters and made many tearful trips to the camp sub-office trying to locate the missing members. Success often came by sheer luck and not through any set procedure. It was chaos all around. There were heartbreaking scenes prior to June when busloads of people who walked out of the war zone arrived in the camps. People in the camps would run behind these buses hoping to catch a glimpse of a missing relative. If someone in the bus waved at them, there would be endless speculation about whom the wave was directed at and who the person was. These were all signs of a longing that family members who were not already in the camp had survived and made it across.

It was these people suffering intense anxieties about friends and families who were brutally stopped by the military from entering adjacent camps to check if the missing loved one had arrived there. The number of times inmates were brutally beaten when caught attempting to cross from one camp to another was countless. The camps were full of stories on how even women were beaten up. Walking down the gravel road that separated Zone 2 and Zone 3 camps, one could see the barbed wire had been breached at several places, where determined people had made spaces to cross over. The military would, at gunpoint, gather young men to mend these breached places, but people kept breaching them again and again.

The military also separated families by taking away people suspected of LTTE membership or association as the people were making their way across from the war zone. Trying to locate the whereabouts of such members was the most traumatic. In many cases families did not even know if the family member had perished in Vanni or had been taken away by the military. ICRC played a part in giving information to the families whenever it managed to find out the whereabouts of the missing person. If the names were not on the ICRC list, then locating such cases was impossible. By July, ICRC was prevented from visiting the detention centers where LTTE members and supporters were kept and thus helping with family reunion. Many families were still searching for members in this category when I left the camp.

Contacting family living elsewhere also became an ordeal because most people had lost the addresses and phone numbers during the escape. Possessing a mobile phone was a crime and remained a crime until the time I left the camp.

If there was any doubt that the Manik Farm camps were anything other than prisons, the procedure in place for outside visitors to meet detainees will clear away that doubt. Each zone had a space allocated where outsiders must come to seek face to face meetings with inmates. There were times when they were barred from bringing anything to be given to the inmates. This was relaxed later. The visitor gave a piece of paper to the personnel manning the place, with the names of the inmates they wished to meet. This would be announced over the public announcement system. Not all the tents in the camp were within audible limits of this announcement system. By the time the inmate heard the announcement and took the long trek to the meeting place, anything from one to two hours would have passed. Across a divide, separated by barbed wire, the inmates and visitors had to identify and signal to each other that they would enter the meeting area on the next turn. A fixed number of inmates (around fifty in Zone 3) were permitted into the meeting area at a time, and their corresponding visitors were also then permitted in. The actual meeting area was divided by iron sheets up to the chest, and above it were wooden grills similar to what one would find in a prison. The visitors and inmates could talk through this grill and also exchange items over the grill. One was permitted only around twenty minutes maximum to talk because there would be hundreds more waiting. Even within this short time, one was often interrupted by the military demanding the national identity card of the visitor and details about their relationship to the inmate. The waiting area for the Zone 3 visitors had no shade and they would be waiting in the burning sun for hours.

Crowning the suffering of the people was the sadism of the military. I witnessed instances where the beating by the military was purely for sadistic pleasure. Once I saw an old man just squatting on the Zone 3 side of the gravel road watching through the barbed wire the goings on in Zone 2. A military person walking past called the old man on to the road and started beating him. It was clear to me that the beating was purely for sadistic pleasure. In another instance, a medical employee inmate was regularly carrying some refrigerated medicines from one outpatient clinic to another inside the same camp. The employee used a short cut through the tents instead of using the longer gravel road. One Lankan Military duo on a motorbike attempted to stop the employee, suspecting that he was selling the goods. (Camp dwelling sellers tried to buy wares from the wholesale Sinhalese vendors and walk around the camp to resell it for a small profit. The military prohibited this and treated them like criminals.) The hospital employee in question failed to stop because he never suspected that he was the target of the military order to stop. The angered military duo drove their motorbike through the narrow space between the tents, bringing down clothes that were hanging on strings stretched cross the tents, and endangering young children playing in there. They reached the employee, who was now just in front of my tent, stopped and got off the motorbike and walked angrily towards him shouting something in Sinhalese. The Tamil employee, who did not understand Sinhalese, kept repeating "hospital... hospital", which is a word most of the people in world would understand. (Indeed 95 percent of the inmates, all of whom were Tamils, did not understand Sinhalese; whereas 99 percent of the military, all of whom are Sinhalese, did not know Tamil and gave their orders as "masters" in Sinhalese, which the "slaves" did not understand.) The enraged military man kicked the employee in his face and stomach several times with his boots while the employee kept repeating "hospital... hospital". It was only after the military man was too tired to deliver any more kicks that he stopped to look at what was in the box that the employee was carrying. Several of us witnessed this in close quarters, frozen in fear. When the scene cleared, I asked one senior government employee inmate if this misconduct by the military ought to be reported. I was told that if I attempted anything like that I would "disappear".

Rumors of dead bodies floating in the river adjacent to the camp and disappearances continuously spread among the camp community. It was difficult to ascertain the facts behind these rumors. I also heard people talk about women in the camp prostituting to the military in exchange for food. This often happened along the edge of the camp nearer to the residence of the military. Young women flirting with the military were also a very common sight in the camp, and it is a good guess that the women were after food, which the military could readily provide.

There were people whom the camp inmates called "CIDs". They were apparently senior LTTE members who had been taken away and then "released" into the camp to be with their families. Their job was to spot LTTE members and LTTE police who had not reported to the military. One such CID man was living close to my tent. I saw him interrogating other men suspected of close liaison with the LTTE. This CID man had apparently said that he would do this after he was tortured until he agreed.

Until the end of May, until the last of the displaced had arrived, most people talked a lot about who had been killed since they had left. Stories of entire families being killed were common in the conversations of the inmates. Especially when extended families or people from the same locality met for the first time since getting out of the war zone, they had numerous stories to share about the fate of unfortunate relatives and villagers. How best to trace missing relatives was always part of this topic of conversation. Descriptions of the experience of crossing over from the war zone were described in minute detail by those who had crossed over in March. While crossing over, people faced intense fears of being shot at either by the military or by the LTTE. Families often got separated when they were fired at. Wealthier people hired boats to cross over. One mother lost all of her four children when her boat was fired at by the military, suspecting it to be an LTTE boat.

Those who arrived in May described the experience of the last few days of the war in great detail. Many said that during the last few days they never walked erect due to fear of being hit by shelling. When making the move to exit the area, they said that they had to walk over dead bodies.

Other topics included the amount of money they had wasted in transporting their possessions as they displaced again and again in Vanni. The loss of their entire possessions was acutely felt and discussed over and over again. When feeling a little less tense, the inmates never tired of describing their yard and all the trees and vegetables that would be growing there. The soothing shade of large mango and jack trees in their yards were frequently remembered and contrasted with the lack of shade from the scorching sun in the camp.

The goings on in the camp itself also dominated the conversation of inmates who were living near each other. The most common topic was the fights among inmates that always took place at the water collection queues. These fights, indicative of the tension caused by competition for the limited availability of water, created a very bad atmosphere among the inmates, who were otherwise very amicable and helpful to each other.

The New Zealand High Commissioner for Sri Lanka in Delhi made efforts to get me out of the camp, but for four months he could not make any progress. A friend obtained a release on the basis of my over-sixty status, but that was cancelled by the defense ministry in Colombo. By this time I realized that I had little chance of being released officially, and I got out by "other" means and managed to arrive in New Zealand.

By December 2009, the majority of the inmates were allowed to go back to their homes, but many thousands remained in the camps. Even the resettlement of the people released from the camps continued to remain inadequate and controversial. Some of the camp inmates who went back to their original villages in Jaffna were harassed and even tortured by Lankan-sponsored paramilitaries. I know of some who secretly went back to Manik Farm camp for security.

16

No nation
is an island

On arrival in New Zealand, I struggled to recollect the memories of Vanni and the people I had come to know. I began the long and painful process of finding out what had happened to the hundreds of people I had worked with and cared about. Because of the destruction and dispersion of community networks, this was turning out to be a never-ending process. I located some; some are dead; some are maimed; some escaped the island; and some have disappeared. In Vanni I had recorded stories of people who had disappeared between 1990 and 2008. It was now my turn to feel that heartwrenching pain of curtailed grief. Every living member of the Eelam Tamil community had experienced this trauma over the disappearance of someone they knew. A three-year old-child close to my heart was among the many I knew who disappeared after walking out of Mullivaikaal.

The vast majority of Eelam Tamils, even those who had been strong critics of the LTTE, felt a great sense of loss because abruptly they were made to look into a future that was a vacuum. With the all pervasive presence of the LTTE removed, everyone re-evaluated their view on Tamil nationalism, while also being burdened by the humanitarian catastrophe facing those who walked out of the war zone. The analysis of the defeat of the LTTE dominated Eelam Tamil thought for one year. The LTTE's lack of political acumen; its inability to gain friends in the international scene; the clever military strategies of the Lankan government; new international alliances forged by the Lankan government; the Lankan government's no-turning-back war footing; defection by Eastern Batticaloa LTTE leader Karunaa; the peace process and the resulting opening up causing loss of intelligence protection for the LTTE; and an international plot to destroy the LTTE were all put forward as theories for the LTTE defeat, and indeed all of them had a grain of truth. Of these factors only the first two were in LTTE's control. There were external conditions that stopped the LTTE from forging friendly alliances as outlined below. If this was a given, then did the LTTE lack the political acumen to see this situation and take appropriate actions? That is something Tamils will need to reflect on for years to come.

The post-May 2009, post-Mullivaikaal scenario has provided some useful lessons for those who care to read them. The public crystallization of factions among international players is particularly educative. The immediate reaction of the international players can only be described as a black comedy, congratulating the Lankan government for eradicating terrorism. The UN Human Rights Council, especially, discredited itself gravely in this respect by passing a resolution on 27 May 2009, immediately after the end of war, congratulating the Lankan government.[24] Political games inside the UN Security Council also brought into the open the state of international injustice, with China and Russia using their veto power to block any resolution condemning Sri Lanka. The UN panel report of April 2011,[25] by the panel of experts appointed by the UN Secretary General, ameliorated to some extent the black comedy that was being enacted by the international players till then. International players on this issue have publicly crystallized into three factions: India, the pro-Lankan side led by China and Russia, and the West. It is worth studying the positions of each of these groups with respect to the LTTE.

India's interest in the Tamil struggle has two aspects. If the Tamil grievance in the island is not addressed then the large Tamil population in the Indian state of Tamilnaadu will become restless. India also exploited the Tamil grievance as a leverage to keep the anti-Indian sentiments of the Sinhala majority in the Lankan government in check. India had assisted in the training Tamil militants during the early 1980s in the very early stages of the Tamil armed struggle. Once the LTTE established itself as dominant among the Tamil militant groups, India found that the LTTE could not be corrupted and manipulated to meet India's interests. The LTTE remained steadfast in its goal of an independent state of Tamil Eelam which India saw as a threat to its unity and security. An incorruptible armed rebel movement in its backyard is a threat to any state oppressing its own minorities and its lower castes. India became and remained antagonistic towards the LTTE. The war between the LTTE and the Indian forces during the late 1980s was not the cause but rather an outcome of this antagonism.

The people of the state of Tamilnaadu within India with its large Tamil population share a common heritage with the people of Tamil Eelam. They are the LTTE's natural ally. But due to pan-Indian objections whatever support that existed within Tamilnaadu was minimised. Yet, the LTTE viewed India as its potential long term ally despite pan-Indian antagonism. I was able to observe this firsthand in Vanni. I am certain the LTTE would not have formed any alliance that would put the wider security interests of India at risk. Thus seeking Chinese assistance was never in the LTTE's calculations. It is worth noting that the Chinese ambassador was the first foreign diplomat to visit the LTTE after the 2002 ceasefire.

I am also convinced that the LTTE ideology would have prevented it from entering into any negotiated alliance with another state. Such an alliance would have involved compromises to the sovereignty of Tamil Eelam. A common refrain in LTTE discourses in Vanni was that they depend on no one but the Eelam Tamil people to wage their struggle. The influential Tamil Diaspora living in the West also would have resisted the LTTE making alliances with states that would be seen as against the interests of the West. The LTTE did seek support from the newly born states of East Timor and Eritrea for reasons of shared interest in struggles of similar nature. I am not sure about the extent of support these weak states could have provided.

China has risen as an economic power in the post cold-war era. It has actively sought economic influence in many parts of the globe including Africa and the South Pacific. There was no doubt that China was eager to exploit the ceasefire atmosphere in the island to gain an economic foothold. When the 2002 ceasefire began to break down from 2006 onwards, the West began to put pressure on Lanka to respect the ceasefire clauses. In order to balance this pressure, Lanka welcomed large scale Chinese involvement. Prominent among the Chinese projects is the Hambantota harbour in southern coast of the island. Many analysts say that this is a pearl in the "string of pearls" project by China to protect its oil supply routes from the Middle East and prevent US/NATO dominance in the Indian Ocean. Lanka also received large Chinese military supplies. Several other pro-China states also swelled this pro-Lanka faction.

Despite this background isolation, the growth and strength of the LTTE was unmistakable. The position of the West regarding the LTTE therefore deserves further study. In the post May 2009 era, a strong push for war crimes charges against the Lankan Military was evident. Publicly this is led by a group of three organizations, Amnesty International, Human Rights Watch, and the International Crisis Group. Their efforts are backed by the UK's Channel 4 television. The Channel 4 documentary, *Sri Lanka Killing Fields,*[26] which shows only a fraction of the calamity visited on the Tamil people, became a tool for their push for a war crimes investigation. Their input was also visible in the UN panel report of April 2011. It is safe to assume that this group is working with similar, if not the same, goal with respect to this issue. Demanding war crime investigations of the Lankan government has been their main platform in the post-Mullivaikaal period.

This post-Mullivaikaal position of the West provides a unique chance for Tamils and others who have also followed closely the LTTE campaign over the previous decades, to gain deep insight into contemporary international relations. What did the group, Amnesty International, Human Rights Watch, and International Crisis Group, focus on during the pre-May 2009 period? These include: a long list of charges against the LTTE; some charges against members of the Tamil Diaspora, which have been extended into the post-May 2009 period; and a negative position on the independent state of Tamil Eelam. Given that similar sentiments were also raised by the US government and other Western bodies, it is safe to conclude that this was at this time the position of the Western block on these issues.

During the pre-May 2009 period, the Western block conducted an aggressive campaign against the LTTE. Its child soldier campaign was the most vigorous and incessant. Assassinations of political leaders and Tamil collaborators and civilians in Colombo were the next strongest condemnations that the LTTE faced. Its authoritarian rule in the areas it controlled came in for complaint, along with frequent allegations that the international wing of LTTE engaged in money extortion, people smuggling, drug trafficking, and credit card fraud. Like many Tamil Diaspora activists I, too, was caught up in and was personally affected by this anti-LTTE international campaign.[27]

Overlapping this period of LTTE violations, there was a litany of even more brutal Lankan violations. These Lankan violations have been recorded extensively, not by these Western groups, but only by Tamil groups, including NESoHR. It is plain to see the extreme bias in the condemnations expressed by the Western block in general and the group of three organizations mentioned above in particular. Extremely important lessons can be learnt by keenly studying the contrast in the positions of the Western block pre and post Mullivaikaal times.

Take the period after May 2009. Not long after the final collapse of the LTTE, the International Crisis Group charged that the violence may be reignited because the Tamil Diaspora had not given up the LTTE ideology.[28] This was the charge against a transnational community that had just faced one of the gravest traumas of the century. Why was such an accusation made? In fact International Crisis Group has the stated policy of proactively disputing claims for an independent state in only two of the numerous such conflicts in the world.[29] One of the two claims they are against is that of the Eelam Tamils and the other is that of the Kurds. This group of three organizations, and by implication the West, continues to criticize the Tamil Diaspora for promoting an independent state of Tamil Eelam. Why this is so?

The Western block has pursued an unbalanced policy of discrediting the LTTE, picking on every slippage in its conduct while ignoring the decades of Lankan government atrocities to which the LTTE was reacting. Furthermore, the Western block denies outright the right to secede, despite repeated demonstrations that no other just resolution is possible. It accuses the Tamil Diaspora for thinking about seceding even while it was recovering from the May 2009 Genocide. All these networks of state interests are riddles which Tamils must solve.

An awareness of nature and the environment has brought terms like ecosystem and biosphere into mainstream discourse. It tells us of the interdependence of all living things, which in turn depend on the earth and its atmosphere. There is a similar interdependence created in human military and politico-economic affairs at the global level, but no mainstream discourse seeks to raise public awareness about it as this might lead to public intervention to stop the evil that states do. Tamils can resolve the riddles thrust in their face only by grasping this interdependent global politico-military-economic sphere and its decisive influence on the outcome of the LTTE campaign.

The LTTE erred many times and in many ways, but it definitely was not the ruthless armed group rhetorically repeated by the Western block. The latest rhetoric even includes a confident assertion that "the world is a better place without the LTTE."[30] The LTTE fought a ruthless state alone, with only the support of the Tamil Diaspora and without the support of any other state. Despite this, it was the most successful armed group in moving towards its goal. It almost succeeded in taking on the world. This was the most unsettling feature of LTTE—it was the sheep that learned to open the gate, and thus must be shot. Many other nations have achieved their goal of independence without making even one hundredth of the sacrifices made by the Tamils. They succeeded not because their liberation movement was better, but because the politico-military-economic conjunction was conducive—because powerful states wanted it to happen, in short.

Impressive social changes occurred in the Vanni under LTTE. What Gandhi, Ambedkhar, and Periyaar failed to achieve in India, the LTTE achieved in Vanni. The pervasive caste-consciousness of South Asia was eliminated. Vanni held the promise of progressive ideals for women in the society and of a government oriented toward the well being of the people. Infusing people with the spirit of struggle, it united them as one people. Indeed, it held the promise for many more social changes that would have benefited Tamils and perhaps even the whole of South Asia. This powerful example has now been destroyed. Even if an independent Tamil Eelam state is miraculously born in future, it will not bring back that hope and that promise that Vanni once held.

I will conclude this book by citing a poem. Baarathiyaar, a famous Tamil poet, wrote this during the Indian independence struggle. I cry for Vanni every time I read this because it so perfectly captures the emotions of Eelam Tamils.

Freedom crop

Not water that nourished
This crop—Oh God Almighty!
We cherished it with our tears
You now desire it burnt

To turn dreams to reality
We grew within our soul
This kaleidoscope lamp
You now wish to put out

After a thousand years
Of lifeless existence
Came this rare gem
Are we now to lose it

Parted from families
By vulgar cruelty
Less their romance—our youth
You see not their loss

The great languish
In brutal prisons
The learned in hard labor
You see not their pain

The finest among us
Their heart in deep anguish
Like a blind child
Their cry you do not hear

சுதந்திரப் பயிர்

தண்ணீர் விட்டோ வளர்த்தோம்
சர்வேசா இப்பயிரை
கண்ணீரால் காத்தோம்
கருகத் திருவுளமோ

எண்ணமெல்லாம் மெய்யாக
எம்முயிரினுள் வளர்ந்த
வண்ண விளக்கிது
மடியத் திருவுளமோ

ஒராயிரம் வருடம்
ஒய்ந்து கிடைந்த பின்னர்
வராது போல் வந்த
மாமணியை தோற்போமோ

மாதரையும் மக்களையும்
வண் தன்மையால் பிரிந்து
காதல் இளைஞர்
கருத்தழிதல் காணாயோ

மேலோர்கள் வெஞ்சிறையில்
வீழ்ந்து கிடப்பதுவும்
நூலோர்கள் செக்கடியில்
நோவதுவும் காண்கிலையோ

எண்ணற்ற நல்லோர்
இதயம் புழுங்கி இரு
கண்ணற்ற சேய் போல்
கலங்குவதும் காண்கிலையோ

Appendix

A brief history

The island of Sri Lanka was populated by humans for more than 100,000 years.[31] The present day population of approximately 20 million falls into four broad ethnic groups. These are majority Sinhalese (appox.74%); Eelam Tamils (approx.13%); Muslims (approx. 7%), and Upcountry Tamils (approx. 6%).[32] Upcountry Tamils, the last group to arrive on the island 200 years ago, also speak the same Tamil language as the Eelam Tamils. They live in the highlands in the middle of the island. They were brought over to the island from India by the British colonialists to work in the tea plantations. Muslims arrived prior to the colonial period as traders. Until the escalation of the conflict in the 1980s, the majority of the Muslims on the island also used the Tamil language in their homes. This began to change as the conflict intensified. Today, Muslims speak the majority language of the region where they live. In Tamil-dominated regions, they speak Tamil, and in Sinhala-dominated regions they speak Sinhalese. Both these groups, the Upcountry Tamils and Muslims, were also drawn into, and affected by, the ethnic conflict in the island.

The ethnic conflict on the island is mainly between the Sinhala and the Eelam Tamil people, whose roots date back many millennia. Tracing Tamil roots is controversial because it is buried in the Buddhist myths of the majority Sinhala people. The conflict is therefore fought not only at the political level but also at the academic level among historians. Thus, history is part and parcel of the conflict and the reader should be very aware of this.

The ancient people of the island were separated from southern India only by a very narrow strait, which could be crossed in manual boats. Thus exchanges of trade, culture, language, and people existed all through the human history of this region.[33] When Buddhism spread to the region, it thrived on the island but faded away in India. Eventually it also faded away from parts of the island closest to southern India. During this phase, due to the influence of Buddhism, a new language, Sinhala, developed in the south of the island, and the Tamil language of southern India flourished in the parts closest to it. Thus, by default, the people who spoke the Sinhalese language adhered to Buddhism, and people who spoke the Tamil language adhered to the Hinduism of southern India.

Beginning in the 16th century, for more than four centuries, the island came under three consecutive colonial powers. The three colonial powers on their arrival found many smaller kingdoms and chieftainships on the island. The first to arrive were the Portuguese who managed to control only the coastal regions of the island. People in the coastal regions converted to Catholicism due to the missionary work carried out under the Portuguese rule. Today Catholics represent about 7 percent of the island population, and they can be found among both Sinhala and Eelam Tamil people. The Dutch colonial powers ousted the Portuguese approximately one hundred years later. The Dutch, too, failed to make further inroads into the island. Britain took over from the Dutch and managed to bring the entire island under their control by 1815. Protestant Christianity arrived with British missionaries and was embraced by a minority among both Sinhala and Eelam Tamil people.

In 1931, Ceylon, as the island was called then, gained universal franchise. In 1948, Ceylon gained independence from Britain. As the British rule drew to a close from 1915-1946, ethnic politics was already heating up. Tamil resistance to Sinhala domination was already visible. Dismissing this early Tamil dissent, the British rulers drafted a constitution for a centralized government for the independent Ceylon. This centralized constitution is the primary reason for the conflict between Tamils and Sinhalese. Prior to colonialism, despite the ebb and flow of power, some degree of separation was maintained between Tamils and Sinhalese. This was noted in the records of the early colonialist, the Portuguese.

In his analysis of militant Buddhism in Lanka,[34] Tambiah says the seed of this militant Buddhism appeared during the British rule from 1860-1915. Buddhist anger was initially directed against the colonialists and other aliens. The Muslims, who controlled trade in the island at that time, were another target of Buddhist anger. Tambiah's book, published in 1992 and banned in Lanka, traces the political developments on the island from British colonial rule. What follows is a summary of what he wrote. To trace the developments after 1992, I will use a paper by Velupillai.[35]

The very first government of independent Ceylon, during its very first year itself, disenfranchised the Upcountry Tamils, who gained their right to vote through the universal franchise of 1931. This effectively reduced the Tamil vote by half. The Tamil struggle for sharing power in Tamil Eelam within a federal setup started soon after with the formation of a new Tamil political party, the Federal Party. It campaigned for a federal constitution for the island that would give limited autonomy in the Tamil homeland where ninety percent of the people were Tamil speaking at the time of independence.

Militant Buddhism now converged with parliamentary politics. Sinhala Buddhist sentiments became a powerful election campaign tool of the Sinhala politicians. The two main Sinhala political parties, the United National Party (UNP) and the Sri Lanka Freedom Party (SLFP) evolved, competing with each other to be more Sinhala Buddhist than the other. This version of Sinhala Buddhism took on an anti-Tamil sentiment.

Due to the preference of the British colonial government to employ minorities, Tamils held the majority of the government administrative jobs at the time of independence. This Tamil dominance also became a tool for whipping up anti-Tamil sentiments. Tamils received the next blow with the introduction of Sinhala Only Language Act in 1956. This act made Sinhala language the only official language of the state. Prior to this, Sinhala, Tamil, and English were all recognized as official languages. The vast majority of Tamils were made illiterate overnight. Tamils, led by the Federal party, launched non-violent protests against this language policy. The protesters were manhandled by the State forces. This was followed by the very first large-scale pogrom against Eelam Tamils in 1958, famously documented by Tarzi Vittachi in his book *Emergency '58*.

Several agreements reached between Tamil and Sinhala politicians to give partial autonomy to the Tamils were abrogated due to opposition among the Sinhalese. In fact, there was a repeating pattern to the agreements and abrogation. Whenever one of the two main Sinhala parties in power reached an agreement with the Tamil party, the other main Sinhala party in opposition would whip up anger among the Sinhalese voters, forcing the party in power to abrogate the agreement. Interspersed among these abrogated agreements were multiple pogroms directed against the Tamils and sanctioned by the government. The pogrom in 1958 was followed by larger and larger pogroms in 1977, 1981, and 1983. (I was part of a project spanning several years to document these and many other massacres of Tamils by the Lankan Military. I describe this in detail in the main text.) In 1981, the public library in the Tamil-dominated city of Jaffna was burnt down by Sinhala thugs assisted by the Lankan government forces. A large collection of irreplaceable manuscripts, considered to be the second largest such collection in South Asia, was destroyed.[36]

In 1971, Sri Lanka instituted a system of university admission that was seen by the Tamils as discriminatory. The Tamil youth, disadvantaged by this new system of admission, felt further alienated. Some consider this to be a push factor for the youth to become militant. In 1972, Ceylon became a republic, shedding the last of its colonial ties with Britain. Ceylon also got its current name, Sri Lanka, together with the new constitution. The new constitution recognised Buddhism as a State religion. The constitution was again redrafted in 1978 with another which replaced the older Westminster style parliamentary system with an all powerful executive presidency. Even though Eelam Tamils have been making their political aspirations for power sharing clear in each of the general elections, both these constitutions ignored Tamil political aspirations.

Tamils frustrated by lack of progress in their political struggle came together in 1976 to declare the now famous *Vaddukkodai Resolution,* which demanded an independent state of Tamil Eelam. In the subsequent general election, the combined Tamil parties campaigned based on this resolution and received a resounding mandate for it. Velupillai writes, "The Tamil demand to 'leave them alone' was a way of giving notice that if the centralized unitary Sinhala Buddhist framework could not be dismantled, the Tamil people would use their sovereignty to establish a separate country. The Sinhalese could not be expected to agree to share the island with Tamils in two independent countries. In fact, they started fighting against an imaginary Tamil country in 1957, even before any Tamil thought of demanding a separate country."

The post-independence history thus far was taking place during the Cold War era of a bipolar world. The island's big neighbor, pro-USSR India, was watching these developments in Sri Lanka, which had remained a Western ally until then. India decided to turn Lanka to its side, and the disgruntled Tamil youths were the ideal means to do it. India trained and armed many Tamil groups. The 1983 island-wide pogroms directed against the Tamils pushed the Tamil armed struggle to the forefront. Tamil youths now joined the various armed groups in larger numbers.

In 1985, in Thimbu, the capital of the tiny kingdom of Bhutan near India, under India's patronage, negotiations were held between the Sinhalese government and Tamil political parties and militant groups. Tamils together put forward four principles as the basis of Tamil political demands. They demanded recognition: 1) of Tamils as a nation and not just a minority; 2) of the homeland of the Tamils; 3) of their right to self-determination; and 4) of the citizenship rights of all Tamil speaking people living on the island, including the Upcountry Tamils who previously had been denied it. The negotiations at Thimbu ended in failure. Tamils by now were convinced that the Lankan government could not be trusted with the security and freedom of the Tamils without its acceptance of these four basic principles. These four principles have since remained as the basis of the Tamil political demands and are referred to as the *Thimbu principles.*

The LTTE emerged as the leader of the Tamil armed struggle either by absorbing or decimating the other groups. Eventually India and Lanka signed the Indo-Lanka accord in 1987. The LTTE refused to accept the accord and India signed it in spite of this on behalf of the Tamils. As part of this accord, India landed a large contingent of Indian troops in the

Tamil homeland. The Indian troops (IPKF - Indian Peace Keeping Force) fought the LTTE and in the process committed large scale massacres and rapes of Tamil civilians. The Sinhala south erupted, also objecting to the presence of Indian troops. The Lankan government and the LTTE held a round of peace talks. Lanka and the LTTE together demanded and achieved the eviction of the Indian troops, claiming that they could solve their problem among themselves. Soon war erupted again between Lanka and the LTTE.

The LTTE won acclaim among Tamils for its military prowess and discipline. Its Black Tiger unit, the suicide squad, aroused awe among the Tamils and caused deep concern in the Western nations. Continued military engagement put pressure on the LTTE for manpower. Many Tamils deserted the island and escaped to Western nations. The LTTE created a massive network among Diaspora Tamils for funds and political work. Locally, the armed struggle ground on, and the Tamils, affected by the brutality of the Lankan Military, became the target population for LTTE recruitment. A new culture was now in place for taking forward the armed struggle.

The Tamil-speaking Muslim population in Tamil Eelam, who took an active part in the earlier non-violent protests of the Tamils, were now becoming alienated from the Tamil political struggle. There was violence in the eastern district of Batticaloa between Muslims and Tamils. Muslim youths armed by the Lankan Military attacked Tamils. There was also violence by the LTTE against the Muslim people in the eastern district. In 1992, probably fearing a similar development in Jaffna in the north, the LTTE ordered the entire Muslim population out of Jaffna with twenty-four hours notice. This was strongly condemned by the world.

People on the island, now tired of the long years of war, voted in a popular female president in 1994 to bring peace. A ceasefire was signed and talks were held between the LTTE and Lankan representatives. The new president presented a new devolution proposal. This was welcomed by the main Tamil political party. Tamils suggested further improvements to it to meet the Tamil aspirations. The LTTE rejected it as too little. There was loud objection among the Buddhist Sinhalese, and the proposals were diluted in response to the Sinhalese objections. The main Tamil political party was disillusioned with the diluted proposals. Objections among the Sinhalese on the other hand continued even against the diluted proposal. Some Buddhist monks threatened to fast unto death in protest.

The efforts of the "peace president", who also had strong Western support, resulted in a "war for peace". The LTTE was accused of breaking the ceasefire agreement. The Lankan Military onslaught evicted the LTTE from its main center in Jaffna in 1995. The entire Jaffna population of more than 400,000 also walked out overnight with the withdrawing LTTE.

Most of this large population settled in Vanni, and the LTTE began its de-facto state project in Vanni with Kilinochchi as its center. The war continued and became a stalemate. Citing child-soldiers and attacks on politicians and civilian targets, the USA and the UK added the LTTE to their lists of terrorist organizations during the late 1990s. A section of the Jaffna population that had walked out of Jaffna with the LTTE began to slowly drift back to Jaffna, which was under Lankan Military rule, because life in Vanni under conditions of war and the Lankan economic embargo was too hard.

Following some major military successes by the LTTE, the Lankan government and the LTTE signed the Norwegian-brokered ceasefire in 2002. The agreement was signed by a West-friendly prime minister from one of the two main Sinhala parties. It was opposed by the female peace president, who was from the other main Sinhala party. She accused the prime minister of failing to consult her before signing the ceasefire agreement.

International peace monitors, the Sri Lankan Monitoring Mission (SLMM), selected from Nordic countries, was set up with two main offices, one in Colombo and one in Kilinochchi, to monitor compliance of the ceasefire agreement by both parties. Two Peace Secretariats were established with Norway's funding—one in Colombo for the Lankan government and another in Kilinochchi for the LTTE.

Six rounds of direct talks took place in 2003 in different cities outside the island. Agreements were reached to institute structures to bring improvements to the living conditions of the war-affected Tamil people. The LTTE accused the Lankan authorities of failing to implement the agreements reached at the direct talks. During the period of the six rounds of direct talks, the donor countries to Sri Lanka held a conference in Tokyo, which was attended by both the Lankan and LTTE representatives. The USA, Japan, EU, and Norway appointed themselves as the Co-Chairs of this donor conference. This group of four, to be referred as the Co-Chairs of the peace process, was to become an important player in the peace process. In a follow up conference held in the USA, the LTTE was not invited because the USA had already proscribed the LTTE as a terrorist group. Eventually, the LTTE withdrew from direct talks in 2004 citing exclusion from the donor conference and non-implementation of agreements reached in the earlier direct talks. Indirect discussions, however, followed on an interim arrangement for rehabilitation of war-affected people.

Both the prime minister and the LTTE put forward proposals for an interim administration to manage the rehabilitation of war-affected people. The prime minister who signed the ceasefire agreement and the LTTE again agreed to hold direct talks in a city outside the island to discuss the proposals. Just prior to this proposed talk, the peace president dissolved parliament, forcing the talks to be cancelled. Elections were called in April 2004. Just prior to this election, the LTTE faced the defection of its top eastern commander, who soon afterwards joined the Lankan government, which appointed him as a member of parliament. The prime minister who signed the ceasefire agreement lost the parliamentary election, thus bringing in the hardline opponents, who were against the ceasefire agreement. From then until the end of the war, the president, the cabinet and its prime minister were all from the same hardline alliance. The party of the Prime Minister that signed the 2002 ceasefire agreement did not regain power.

In 2004, on request from the international peace facilitators, a human rights body, North East Secretariat on Human Rights (NESoHR), was established in Kilinochchi to strengthen the peace process. The December 2004 tsunami, which wrought havoc along the eastern borders of the island, affected both the Sinhala and the Tamil people. Massive international aid was promised to assist in the rehabilitation following this disaster. The Lankan government blocked most of this aid reaching the people in the LTTE-administered areas. Hopes were raised when another agreement, the Post Tsunami Management Structure (PTOMS), was signed by the Lankan government and the LTTE for the double rehabilitation of war and tsunami-affected Tamil people in Tamil Eelam. This agreement was also facilitated by Norway, but was immediately shelved following a Lankan court order.

The peace process stagnated. Presidential elections were held in November 2005. The female president, held up as the peace president, completed her maximum term of twelve years without bringing peace. The West-friendly prime minister who signed the ceasefire agreement now stood for the presidential elections against a hardline president. The LTTE issued a veiled call for boycotting the presidential elections, saying the Lankan elections were of no concern to the Eelam Tamils. Due to the Tamil boycott, a war president was elected in November 2005, who brought the war to an end in May 2009.

The interested reader can check out the many chronologies available on the web that have been published by reputed bodies.[37]

Endnotes

Foreword

1   'UN Aid Chief Resigns Over Iraq Sanctions' *The Independent* (Thursday 01 October 1998) Patrick Cockburn reporting from Jerusalem.

2   Although the book does not refer to global economic interests it may be noted that the World Bank and the Asian Development Bank agreed to finance the reconstruction and development of the Tamil homeland under the peace plan brokered by Norway and also that Singapore and the Indian government had expressed interest in a 'Tamil Corridor' for IT industries stretching from Malaysia to Tamil Nadu and Karnataka states in India.

A Fleeting Moment in the History of My Country

1   Tamil people on whose behalf LTTE waged its war do not have a unique name to denote them. The name "Tamil" may refer to people in many regions of the world, all of whom do not identify with the Tamil people in question. Since this particular Tamil community does not have a unique name for the region they claim as homeland, they cannot also be referred to with such a regional name. Eelam is a name loosely used, but it is a Tamil name that refers to the entire island. Thus, what has come to be commonly used is the name Tamil Eelam to denote the region claimed as homeland. Unfortunately, this name brings up the notion of a separate state of Tamil Eelam and does not readily permit one to use it simply as a unique name to denote the region. But it is with this meaning that this name will be used here because a name is needed to write about this subject matter.

2   *Impact of Armed Conflict on Children,* 1996, Graca Machel, UNICEF, http://www.unicef.org/graca/ (Last accessed in March 2012). This report by Graca Machel on the "Impact of Armed Conflict on Children" was commissioned by the UN Secretary General. It drew attention to the need to protect children caught in armed conflict and emphasized the interrelated issues that affect children in armed conflict.

3   *Foot prints in sand – M-A-M report,* 2005, NESoHR, http://www.nesohr.org/inception-sept2007/human-rights-reports/MAM-Report-A4N.PDF (Last accessed in March 2012). This report on large-scale disappearances in 1990 in three islets, Mandaitheevu, Allaippiddi, and Mankumbaan, off Jaffna, was investigated and written by me.

4   *Forced eviction of Tamils from Northeast by Sri Lankan armed forces,*
        2005, NESoHR, http://www.nesohr.org/inception-sept2007/human-rights-
        reports/ForcedEvictions-Jaffna.pdf (Last accessed in March 2012). This
        report on the High Security Zones and Forced Eviction in Jaffna prior to
        the 2002 ceasefire was written by me based on the statistics collected
        by the Statistical Centre for North East (SNE).

5   *Lest We Forget Part 1*, 2007,NESOHR, http://www.nesohr.org/files/
        Lest_We_Forget.pdf (Last accessed in March 2012). This report de-
        scribing the large-scale massacres of Tamils from 1956 until 2002 was
        written by me based on the information collected and recorded in Tamil
        by the Statistical Centre for North East (SNE).

6   *Lest We Forget Part 2*, 2008, NESOHR, http://www.nesohr.org/files/
        Lest_We_Forget-II.pdf (Last accessed in March 2012). This report de-
        scribing the large scale massacres of Tamils from 2004 until 2008 was
        collected and written by me.

7   *Statistics on civilians affected by war in Northeast*, 2006, NESoHR, http://
        www.nesohr.org/inception-sept2007/human-rights-reports/StatisticsOnCi-
        viliansAffectedByWar.pdf (Last accessed in March 2012). This report on
        pre-2002 war statistics was written by me based on the statistics collected
        by the Statistical Centre for North East (SNE).

8   *Piramanthanaru massacre*, 2006, NESoHR, http://www.nesohr.org/
        inception-sept2007/human-rights-reports/PiramanthanaruMassacre1985.
        pdf (Last accessed in March 2012). This report on a particular large scale
        massacre in 1985 was written by myself based on interviews conducted
        by me.

9   *Reluctant Mercenary*, 2002, Tim Smith, Book Guild Limited, UK

10   *Fishing communities of Northeast and Ethnic factor*, 2006, NESoHR, http://
        www.nesohr.org/inception-sept2007/human-rights-reports/NorthEastFish-
        ing.pdf (Last accessed in March 2012). This report on the erosion of
        the rights of the Tamil Fishing Community was written by me based on
        interviews conducted by myself.

11   *Demographic changes in the Tamil homeland in the island of Sri Lanka-
        over the last century,* 2008, LTTE Peace Secretariat, http://www.sangam.
        org/2008/05/Demographic_Changes.pdf (Last accessed in March 2012).
        This report on the demographic changes on the island was written by
        myself using information available in other reports in Tamil.

12   *Extrajudicial, summary or arbitrary executions*, Report of the Special
        Rapporteur, Philip Alston, MISSION TO SRI LANKA, (28 November
        to 6 December 2005) http://daccess-dds-ny.un.org/doc/UNDOC/GEN/
        G06/121/17/PDF/G0612117.pdf?OpenElement (Last accessed in March
        2012)

13   *The SLMM report 2002-2008, The Operation – The Organisation,* 2010,
        Norwegian Ministry of Foreign Affairs, http://www.slmm-history.info/
        filestore/slmm_report_101029_final.pdf , (Last accessed in March 2012).
        See the section on "Key events and Developments" for year 2003 when
        the head of SLMM was changed twice.Also see: http://www.tamilnet.com/
        art.html?catid=13&artid=10681 (Last accessed in March 2012)

14   Children and armed conflict in the Northeastern Part of the Island of Sri
        Lanka, 2006, Child Protection Authority, LTTE Peace Secretariat, http://
        www.crin.org/docs/ltte_cac.pdf (Last accessed in March 2012). This
        report on LTTE child soldiers was written by me based on observations
        and interviews conducted by myself.

15   Many Tamils have asked me if I met the LTTE leader Pirapaaharan. I have
        never requested a meeting with him, though Pulitheevan told me on more

than one occasion that I should meet him. I, however, did see Pirapaaharan twice. Once it was in December 2005 when the body of the slain Batticaloa Member of Parliament, Joseph Pararajasingam, was brought to Kilinochchi. I was with the entourage with Kili-father, which received his body at the border. The body was placed in a hall in Kilincochchi, and as the night drew close, most of the people there were asked to leave. There were only a handful of people left, including Parajasingam's family members. Pulitheevan came to me and said I should wait. I was confused. Soon Pirapaaharan arrived with his entourage, paid his last respects to Pararajasingam, chatted with his family briefly and left. Later Pulitheevan asked me if I spoke to Pirapaaharan and when I said I did not, he looked very disappointed. The next time I saw Pirapaaharan was in 2006 at the opening ceremony of the new Senchoolai abode in Kilinochchi. Janani invited me to the opening ceremony, and I foolishly thought it will be like all other such ceremonies. When I went there, I found that everyone was put through a very thorough search. It was then that it dawned on me that Pirapaaharan, too, was going to attend the opening ceremony. When I saw the level of checking, I was inclined to leave the place without attending the ceremony, but I had no transport of my own and I was forced to stay and go through it. My body and footwear were carefully checked. My wristwatch and pen were taken away and handed back at the end of the ceremony. Accidentally, I also sat in the row behind Pirapaaharan and his wife Mathivathani. With the view to please Pulitheevan, I asked Mathivathani to introduce me to Pirapaaharan, and when she did we exchanged a few polite words.

16   Black Tigers: In 2008, following the assassination of Thamilselvan, I heard that many members whom I had come to know well had applied to become Black Tigers, and some of them had been accepted. I was able to meet only one of them, after she was accepted into the Black Tiger division. I also met two more Black Tigers, who had joined the division earlier. I had also heard other LTTE members talk about their friends who had become Black Tigers. From what I could gather from all of this, they all appeared very normal people. All of them cared deeply about their families. People around them had a special feeling for them, but it was not openly displayed. In that context and culture, it did not seem very unnatural to be a Black Tiger. It seemed natural for particular types of personalities subjected to particular emotions as a result of particular circumstances.

Most of the Black Tigers I have known or I have heard about have stood out from the rest in two aspects. Everyone with some maturity knows that people do not all necessarily care for others around them to the same degree. One can observe this all too obviously, even within the same family. I noticed that the Black Tigers in general showed greater concern for others around them, including their families. The other aspect that I noticed was that most of them had suffered a tragedy at the hands of the enemy that had profoundly affected them. As I tried to discern a common thread connecting the Black Tigers that I came to know or heard about from their friends, I was able to observe these two common traits.

17   NESoHR website with all other reports :http:// www.nesohr.org (Last accessed in March 2012)

18   Shortened version of the *White Van* documentary about abductions and disappearances, which I helped to produce in 2006 can be viewed at: http://www.youtube.com/watch?v=ODQxoDnMhis (Last accessed in March 2012)

19   A shortened version of the documentary *Kfir Fodder*, on the bomb-
        ing of a small fishing village in 2007, which I helped to produce, with
        interviews conducted by me can be viewed at: www.youtube.com/
        watch?v=Ph0Cw1mAgAI (Last accessed in March 2012)
20   A shortened version of the documentary, *Madhu Amma*, on the claymore
        attack on a school bus in 2008, which I helped to produce can be viewed
        at: www.youtube.com/watch?v=s1kRdTm-1T0 (Last accessed in March
        2012)
21   A shortened version of the documentary, *Bomber returned*, on the bombing
        of the village Kiranchi in 2008, which I helped to produce can be viewed
        at: www.youtube.com/watch?v=X_zKetfLv6A (Last accessed in March
        2012)
22   *Vanni Bombing and shelling victims since November – released 2 De-
        cember*, 2008, NESoHR, http://www.nesohr.org/files/November_vic-
        tims_of_bombing_and_shelling.pdf (Last accessed in March 2012).
        This report I wrote included a picture of a cluster bomb immediately after
        it was dropped on 29 November 2008. Other Tamil media channels also
        reported it.
        The use of cluster bombs during the war was continuously reported only
        in the Tamil media channels but was not picked up by any international
        media. This pattern of atrocities known and accepted as fact by the Tamils
        but ignored by the international community has been the ongoing story of
        the Eelam Tamil plight for several deades. Curiously, three years later in
        April 2012, a "leaked" email from a UN official involved in demining work in
        Sri Lanka claimed that they have found unexploded cluster munitions. This
        news was immediately followed by further international media reports on
        Tamil victims affected by cluster bombs three years earlier. I find it difficult
        to dismiss these latest "revelations" as anything but stage managed by
        the Western interest groups in the post-war, post-LTTE scenario for war
        crimes charges against the Lankan government. The use of phosphrous
        bombs during the war was another charge that the Tamils have known
        was occurring but was ignored by rest of the world.
23   **White flag incident:** The events between 16-19 May at the end of the
        war are still shrouded in mystery. Large-scale rape, executions, and dis-
        appearances of the Tamil people who walked out of the war zone have
        been widely reported. The UN panel appointed by the UN Secretary
        General released a report on the same topic on 2011. During that last
        phase, some senior LTTE members, including Nadeesan, the Head of
        the political division, and Pulitheevan, the Secretary General of the LTTE
        Peace Secretariat, negotiated their surrender with involvement of the UN
        and Norway. They were instructed to walk towards the Lankan Military
        with a white flag raised high. All of them were shot and killed as they at-
        tempted to surrender with white flag. This incident is now known as the
        "white flag" incident.
24   *The human rights situation in Sri Lanka*, Eleventh Special Session of the
        Human Rights Council: Tuesday 26 and 27 May 2009, http://www2.
        ohchr.org/english/bodies/hrcouncil/specialsession/11/index.htm
        (Last accessed in March 2012)
25   *Report of the Secretary-General's Panel of Experts Report on Accontability
        in Sri Lanka*, 2011, http://www.un.org/News/dh/infocus/Sri_Lanka/
        POE_Report_Full.pdf (Last accessed in March 2012)
26   *Sri Lanka's killing fields*, 2011, UK Channel 4 documentary, http://www.
        channel4.com/programmes/sri-lankas-killing-fields/4od, (Last ac-

cessed in March 2012)

27   Many Tamil activists in New Zealand, including myself, were visited by the Security Intelligence Service (SIS) of New Zealand. Through a member of parliament, I protested the visit to the then Prime Minister of New Zealand. The reply from the prime minister implied that the SIS officer was just paying a friendly visit to keep informed about Tamil community activities. I and other fellow activists certainly did not feel that the visit was friendly. Following my protest, the visits stopped, but other Tamil activists who did not protest continued to have regular visits from SIS.
In March 2003, I was flying from New Zealand to Canada to assist in the care of my ailing mother. This was before my second trip to Vanni in 2004, and I had had no contact with LTTE leadership at that time. My flight to Canada transited through Los Angeles. By accident I ended up in the queue for the airline crew. When the person at the desk hesitated after scanning my passport, I just managed to take a peek at the screen. At the bottom it said, "works for LTTE". I was held back at the airport for more than four hours. The officers were extremely rude, and I was interrogated several times, photographed, fingerprinted, and my baggage was checked minutely. The officers did tell me that I would soon be allowed to proceed with my flight. When night fell, I heard them discussing putting me in a cell outside the airport. I put my foot down and said I would not leave the airport. I told them that they could send me back to New Zealand if they wished, which they did. My mother, who was suffering from renal failure, survived only because she went on dialysis. Since then I made two trips to Canada, taking longer routes to avoid transiting through the USA. However, I was also interrogated at the Canadian airport both times. I was taken aback when even in 2011, the Australian airport authority held me back for an hour before allowing me to proceed.

28   *The Sri Lankan Tamil Diaspora after the LTTE*, 2010, International Crisis Group, http://www.crisisgroup.org/en/publication-type/media-releases/2010/asia/the-sri-lankan-Tamil-diaspora-after-the-ltte.aspx (Last accessed in March 2012).
This report of 2010 warns that the Tamil Diaspora could reignite violence.

29   *Self-Determination and Conflict Resolution: From Kosovo to Sudan*, 2010, Speech by Louise Arbour, International Crisis Group, http://www.crisisgroup.org/en/publication-type/speeches/2010/Louise-Arbour-self-determination-and-conflict-resolution-from-kosovo-to-sudan.aspx (Last accessed in March 2012).
This speech by the head of the International Crisis Group is on the organization's opposition to independence for Tamil Eelam.

30   The phrase, "*World is a better place without LTTE*", was probably started by Gordon Weiss, who is the author of a book on the end war in Sri Lanka. He is also closely associated with the Western push for war crimes investigations. http://www.foreignpolicy.com/articles/2011/04/26/tiger_blood (Last accessed in March 2012).

31   *The Prehistory of Sri Lanka*, 1992, Siran Deraniyagala, Department of Archaeological Survey, Colombo

32   *Demanding Sacrifice: War and Negotiations in Sri Lanka (*chapter on *Historical Context),* 1998, , Elizabeth Nissan, Conciliation Resources, http://www.c-r.org/accord-article/historical-context-accord-sri-lanka, (Last acessed in April 2012)

33   *The Evolution of an Ethnic Identity*, 2006, K Indrapala, Kumaran Book House, Chennai.

34   *Buddhism Betrayed*, 1992, Stanley Tambiah, Chicago University Press.
35   *Sinhala fears of Tamil demands*, 2006, A Velupillai, in *Buddhism, Conflict and Violence in Modern Sri Lanka*, Ed: Mahinda Deegalle, Routeledge.
36   *Destroying a Symbol: Checkered History of Sri Lanka's Jaffna Public Library*, 2006, Rebecca Knuth, World Library and Information Congress—IFLA 2006, Seoul: (http://archive.ifla.org/IV/ifla72/papers/119-Knuth-en.pdf) (Last accessed in April 2012)
37   **Chronologies:**
      Chronology of the Sinhala-Eelam Tamil conflict, 1998, Conciliation Resources, http://www.c-r.org/accord-article/chronology-accord-sri-lanka, (Last accessed April 2012)
      Sri Lanka profile, A chronology of key events, http//www.bbc.co.uk/news/world-south-asia-12004081, (Last accssed April 2012)

CPSIA information can be obtained
at www.ICGtesting.com
Printed in the USA
LVHW021608090720
660248LV00013B/1591

9 780984 525546